THE

DELIGHTS

OF

GROWING

OLD

MAURICE GOUDEKET

Translated from the French by
PATRICK O'BRIAN

The Akadine Press

1996

The Delights of Growing Old

A Common Reader Edition published 1996 by The Akadine Press, Inc.
by arrangement with Farrar, Straus & Giroux, Inc. and Sanda Goudeket.

Originally published in French as *La Douceur de Vieillir.*
Copyright © 1965 by Flammarion.

English translation by Patrick O'Brian copyright © 1966,
renewed 1994, by Farrar, Straus & Giroux, Inc.

ISBN 1-888173-09-2

The Delights of Growing Old

❀

You young people who are frightened at the thought of growing old must learn that there is no happier condition than that of an aged man. Faust was a half-wit who changed his state for yours, and little good it did him. To begin with, let me—I who shall be seventy-five before this book is finished—tell you a secret: it is not really a fact that you grow old at all.

And you, the seventy-five-olds, instead of helping to spread the usual mistaken notion based on mere superficial appearances, as you generally do, you ought to look into your hearts: apart from growing purer and more refined, has the "me" of your first adult years changed in any way? There is shortness of breath, a slowness of movement, a back that will not bend so easily, to be sure, but these are things for our bodies to cope with. The immaterial being that gives our threatened building all its life does not show a single wrinkle, nor will it ever do so.

I know very well that many of you are still disproportionately uneasy about your final exit. One might almost think that death—let's call a spade a spade—has not been at your elbow since you first drew breath. You ought rather to congratulate yourselves on now being safe from the many diseases that only occur in childhood or middle age. A little while ago a friend of mine, a medical man, told me confidentially, "Presently we shall no longer know how to get rid of you people. Pneumonia? Out of the question now; and the same goes for all the infectious diseases. Even your coronary cannot be relied upon. Of course, there's always cancer, but at your age it usually develops so slowly that there is time for you to die of something more agreeable."

For my own part, when the figure 75 happens to force itself upon my attention, my first reaction is astonishment. How can I possibly have got so far? Have I not made some mistake in my reckoning? They tell me I am so absent-minded. What is to be done, where am I to go, and who is going to listen to my complaint? But the next moment I calm down: after all, it is really something of a feat to have lived seventy-five years, in spite of illnesses, germs, accidents, disasters, and wars. And now every fresh day finds me more filled with wonder and better qualified to draw the last drop of delight from it. For up until now I had never known time's inexpressible wealth; and my youth had never entirely yielded itself to happiness. Is it indeed this that they call growing old, this continual surge of memories that comes breaking in on my inner silence, this contained and sober joy, this lighthearted music that bears me up, this wider window on the world, this spreading kindly feeling and this gentleness?

"I have nothing to do today." That is a remark that no longer has any sort of meaning for me. For if it should so chance that I am freed for a while from those everyday duties that by their very monotony give a feeling of emptiness, then so many activities open before me that my only difficulty is choosing between them. With these few free hours of mine in view, thousands of writers have written thousands of books on every conceivable subject, and hosts of artists in every age and country have brought into being a great body of work that the museums have gathered together for my personal benefit. From the earliest recorded time History unrolls, and unrolls for me, its flood of happenings, events so wonderfully wrought up and then resolved that no work of fiction ever reaches such heights of dramatic power and such unexpectedness.

I get up before anyone else in my household, not because sleep has deserted me in my advancing years, but because an intense eagerness to live draws me from my bed. In the same way I drop off every night with a kind of secret satisfaction as I think of the day to come, even if it is likely to be a dark one; for tomorrow is the future and tomorrow contains the whole of that which is possible.

Every morning my breakfast coffee has a fresh taste, and this comes as much from me as it does from the pot. There is the paper too, which will put me in touch with the entire world; and any paper, properly read, has an almost incredible amount of astonishing, moving, ludicrous items in it. Very soon the post will bring me a bill that I had not expected, but it may also bring a touching letter from an unknown correspondent and conceivably—why not indeed?—another from a solicitor telling me that some shatterbrained creature has left me a fortune.

I am surrounded by things, and these things, these

objects, constitute my environment. I am surrounded by people, too, people who mean more to me than my own self—I hear them waking up. The morning's routine is made up of renewing my pact of friendship with these things, these beings, and myself.

Eventually I emerge into the street, and of all wonders, the street is the most wonderful. I do not always approach it the same way. Sometimes I adopt what I call my photographic eye, and then it breaks up into snapshots, set portraits, and groups. Sometimes I look rather for color, and the combinations of color. Sometimes it is hearing that takes precedence over the other senses. But always there are faces, a sea of faces, with everything that they conceal and everything that they give away. I set out, walking, walking, and toward me, surrounding me, there comes this passing show, these unresolved destinies that for a fleeting second brush against my own. At the same moment I feel both united to them and entirely separate. I walk on, on and on, faster and more happily; my senses grow sharper, my thoughts soar up and away, and all the time there is the humming of the great swarm of memories feeding upon my past years, and the mere throbbing of my arteries makes my head swim like wine.

My day has only just begun; I have hardly even begun to reckon up my intangible treasure. "We shall have to leave all this behind," groaned the dying Cardinal Mazarin as he dragged himself through the crowded galleries of his collection. Yet he had lived long enough to learn that anything that is capable of being grasped is also capable of slipping between one's fingers like so much sand. Why did he not turn his fading strength toward those possessions that he could own in a truer sense—a last crowning recollection of his happiest hours, a final human contact, a gleam of sunlight . . .

Most of our memories of childhood and early youth are faked. This is because they come back to us in middle age and toward the end of our life; we grow sentimental about them, and unknowingly we refashion them, giving them a poetic form. We are urged on by the sight of our own children or those we see in the streets and the parks. These rounded, laughing children, as yet untarnished by the slightest stain, their bright faces reflecting new and touching emotions; this childish band, with its ability to set reality to one side and substitute a perpetually re-created world of myth

—here, surely, are the messengers from paradise lost. No doubt they are, but these children will never remember it; it is not this that they will recall. These games, their laughter, and their shouting make up their natural process of living, and there is no reason why any of it should leave a mark. No: what their memory will retain is something of a nature quite unlike these trifling joys—the trace of a deep-rooted sorrow, of some dread or distress, some ghastly discovery.

If I refuse to play false with my memory, it has nothing very edifying to offer. I am perfectly willing to admit that children brought up in the country may be better provided for, because smell is the surest, most faithful sense we possess. "The only one," said Colette, "that will not compromise," and because smells have an incomparable power of calling lost memories to life. It is no doubt possible to reconstitute certain places merely from the scent of crushed leaves or new-mown grass, or even from gently rotting undergrowth or the emanation of a stagnant pond. But practically all the smells that cities give out are unpleasant, and I am wholly and entirely city-bred, having been born in the heart of Paris, in the Saint-Philippe-du-Roule district: rue Frédéric-Bastiat, to be exact. The good smell of hot bread certainly exists in Paris, and I have made use of it in my books, such as they are; but

I have never actually been up early enough to smell it.

I see the first three years of my life as a black hole, sparsely scattered with images. The clearest is still the recollection of my long waits on the balcony of our flat, when I stood watching the house across the way in the hope of seeing the "cocotte" get into her brougham. That is what I heard everyone call her, using a rather shocked tone of voice, which I took for respect. I can still see the coachman and the horse, both of them drowsing, and the whip standing upright in its bucket. Finally "she" appears. The feathers of her boa tremble in the spring breeze. She has an immense hat on her head and a light-colored parasol in her hand: I am already conscious of the dancing grace of her walk. She gets in, the carriage sets off, and I gaze after her as long as I can, listening to the clip-clop of the horse's hoofs dying away in the distance.

This should not be looked upon as anything resembling a precocious inclination, still less as the pointing finger of fate. It is the merest chance that my first memory should make a rather charming little picture. Those which come after it begin that series of covert conflicts with the people around me, the blunderings and the faulty adjustment to my surroundings that make up the unhappiness of every childhood, I am afraid.

How awkward I was at the dawn of the century! Those were the days of the last polkas and the first taxis. I was the same age as the Eiffel Tower, and indeed I was very nearly born at its feet. It so happened that on the night of August 3, 1889, there was a great show in honor of the Shah of Persia at the Exposition. It was there that my mother suddenly felt those pangs of which I alone could be the cause. My parents, protecting the "precious" burden, struggled free of the crowd. Then they had to find a cab, and all this took so much time that my mother was hardly in bed before I appeared, blue in the face and with the cord about my neck, like one of the burghers of Calais—the first of my blunders, and by no means the last I committed in my life, believe me.

The Belle Époque! No doubt it was very gay for some. The iniquitous working of the money system divided society into castes scarcely less rigid than those of India. If you could not put your hand on a twenty-franc piece to tide you over the end of a difficult month, you literally ran the danger of dying of starvation: the solid citizens would not lend one to you, and the others could not. I knew a bank clerk, a married man of thirty, whose weekly spending did not vary by so much as one centime. Every year he saved a sum that would enable him to retire into the country twenty-five years later with an income of six hundred francs.[1] The place had already been chosen, and the budget, which he showed me, had been drawn up in the most approved bookkeeping manner. Had that been my way of expressing grief, I should have burst into tears. The Great War and the inflation that came after it must have reduced my bank clerk to despair, or have shown him the way to levity at last.

My parents, very worthy souls, belonged to that puffed-up lower middle class that would skimp on the essentials and yet consent to any outlay in order to acquire and keep up lifelong connections that would enable them to climb a rung in the social ladder. I still have a dismayed recollection of my mother's grand dinners, in which there were five or six courses, all of a tolerably low quality. The inevitable mock countess sat before the inescapable mock turtle: a poet whose sonnets sometimes found a shelter in remote provincial newspapers—the equivalents of the Gotham *Times* or the Oshkosh *Gazette*—gazed upon a Laodicean dish of chicken that left him neither hot nor cold. A retired general, who had retired often enough when he was on the active list, hung over his *filet de sole Marguery,* dreaming of the intoxication of a charge in battle—an intoxication that had been strangely denied

[1] At that time, about £25 or $125. (Translator)

him. There were generous wines, ruined long since by
their own munificence.

My brother and I (he was a year older) writhed as
we sat. Was it the uncompromisingness of youth that
made us so sensitive to the slightest absurdity? That
and the fact that we were at home in the tragic halls
and palaces of Corneille and Racine, both so very exact in ceremony and splendor. Nothing escaped us.
Our anxious eyes followed the maid, whose clumsiness
was made all the worse by my mother's furious
glances; and we watched the sweating, garlic-breathed
hired waiter, whom we thought far too commonplace
for such a role. My parents drank no wine themselves,
and they looked upon it as a terribly potent beverage
that should only be taken in sips, if that: we also knew
that the two bottles that were meant to satisfy our
guests' thirst would not last the meal, and we went
through exaggerated torments beforehand.

The word "torment" is none too strong, for one of
the first marks of youth is the inability to ascribe relative importance to events. It is not at all a bad thing
that this should be so. One has plenty of time to learn
how to conjugate the verb "to compromise." Reasonable young men reach old age with no spark of fire left
in their hearts.

But this is the reason why one's childhood memories are filled with recollections of wounded pride, made all the worse by damp-handed shyness—a shyness that is based less often upon a feeling of inferiority than upon its opposite. Mine arose from a fear that my worth might not be recognized. It should have been staringly obvious to one and all that I was destined to become the greatest poet of the century, and this should have assured me a reception quite unlike the condescending kindness that I found so offensive. It is true that strangers had not read my five-act tragedy *Frédégonde*, or the sonnet that began:

> *The iron-heavy mere, th' unstirring lake*
> *Lies slumbering deep through its uncounted*
> *   years:*
> *Weary of shining for the labor's sake*
> *The sun no longer lights its leaden tears.*

and ended by comparing the lake with my soul.

Now I come to think of it, lakes made up an important part of my poetical baggage, for my memory provides me with another morsel of "poem":

> *Over the lake, ruffled by the breeze*
> *The swans of anguish glide*
> *Smooth, melancholy, side by side;*
> *Both black and white, rare swans are these.*

One day, whether it was out of daring or long suffering, I summoned up the courage to show my complete works to my mother's first cousin, the poet Gustave Kahn, who asserted that he, rather than Jules Laforgue and Arthur Rimbaud, was the originator of free verse. All he said to me was, "It is not very cheerful." As though poetry should or could be cheerful! I put this coolness down to a low-minded desire to discourage a budding rival, and I returned to my dark brooding.

I did not swallow books: it was books that swallowed me. I had no esteem, of course, for anything but serious books; and my criterion of their seriousness was the degree of their incomprehensibility. It was thus that I read, without skipping a single line, Plato, Locke, Condillac, Spencer, Spinoza, Kant, Hegel, Fichte, Büchner, Boutroux, Poincaré, Auguste Comte, Bergson, the Bhagavad-Gita, various esoteric treatises, and God knows how much else besides. But still this flood of unguided reading did bring with it the *Discourse of Method* and Montaigne's *Essays*.

Millions of words are needed to set up a concept that may not survive longer than a day. Yet nothing one reads is read in vain. Nowadays, thanks to the progress of machines and distribution, young minds, with their uncertain ears and wandering gaze, receive ideas from morning till night. Both choice and judgment are already made for them. If this goes on, what will become of discovery and its possibilities of making happy blunders? Rejecting is just as much a part of the apparatus that sharpens one's mind as accepting. I feel that the essential part of culture lies in the urge to seek it out. Learning on tap fills me with suspicion.

Now here I am, in my very first chapter, committing a serious offense against my own laws. I have just uttered a distinctly unfavorable opinion of the present as compared with the past. That is the very thing that I had promised myself never to do: it is the very thing that *we* ought never to do. Unless you take care, you very soon reach the point of saying, "In my day, my dear sir"—an observation that has the dreariest effect upon others, and one that is exceedingly bad for oneself. As for me, I naturally tend to think the time in which I am living far better than any other, so I do not find this prohibition at all irksome.

Three quarters of a century is by no means more than is needed to struggle free of one's inhibitions. Youth is above all the time for them. They make an integral part of that time of life, and youth's rationalizations are entirely worthless. Mine were the want of an ideal and the absence of adventure. The balance of the world rested upon a notion of the status quo that weighed as heavily as a yoke. At present the reins are too loose; in our parents' days they were too tight. Whatever his own inclinations might be, a son was obliged to follow in his father's footsteps; and a daughter had hardly any more freedom in her choice than she had had in the seventeenth century. Because of this, the young people dawdled through their life as now they dance it. There is nothing that begets boredom so much as too much security.

Except uncertainty, reply the young people of today.

Everything was steady in your time; nothing is in ours. Since you were young, mankind has discovered the secret of destroying itself in less than a second, and now, by way of insuring that it shall survive, it seems to be looking forward to the moment when atomic bombs can be made in the back yard and when any lunatic is able to play with them as he sees fit. At the same time, humanity has pushed the art of healing so far that we are told that presently half the world will be threatened with starvation, so wildly does its population soar—indeed, from now on any forecast about the numbers to be born is more like the announcement of a disaster. An unparalleled churning about among the various colored nations promises to provide us with some quite remarkable mixtures. Violence is setting itself up more or less everywhere: instead of the exception it is becoming the rule, and it is to be found even in the home. There appears to be no point in trying to foresee the future, and hoping to own anything is ludicrous . . .

What of it? I am filled with wonder at living (by what astonishing chance, what kindly stroke of fortune?) at the very height of the crisis in the history of men, the one moment at which it is permissible for them, for the first time in their existence, to put the whole of it into question. The long road I have traveled has primarily taught me that you only cling really passionately to that which you may be about to lose. What period has ever equaled this? With the whole of my curiosity on the stretch and with my antennae rigidly pointed, I eagerly await the outcome. I do not think mankind insane enough to set off the irreparable disaster, nor do I think them wise enough to protect themselves from it; so for me the degree of suspense could scarcely be higher.

In fact, romantic languor, velvet-collared aestheticism, and a passionate addiction to the twist and the Merseyside rhythm are all symptomatic of the same uneasiness in the adolescent, an uneasiness somewhat like that of the fledgling when first it takes to the air. Up until then he was carefully directed, and now all

of a sudden he is on his own, responsible to himself
and to others. Every one of his actions obliges him to
make a choice. At the very time that he acquires physical strength, he is set free to use it upon others, free to
behave well or to behave badly. The smooth run of
his muscles intoxicates and disturbs him; his body fills
him with both delight and anguish. Eager to try out
his new strength, he runs violently against conven-
tions and established lines of conduct. He is alter-
nately tempted to smash the accepted framework and
to seek shelter within it; the herd instinct alternates
with rebelliousness, and often it ends in a haughty
withdrawal.

I was easily offended, much given to daydreaming,
and unspeakably bumptious: there was no possible
refuge for me but solitude. Puberty nearly always
hands a boy over to a kind of anxiety and distress that
is often far greater than his family knows: in my case,
it took on the proportions of a drama. My modesty of
course rose to the splendid height of my other impedi-
ments. When, toward my fourteenth year, a shameful
experience by night disclosed to me my manly state, I
confided in my brother. He was no doubt moved by a
desire to show off, and he dealt with the question so
smuttily that I was shocked and never spoke to him
about it again.

The waking of his senses may lead an adolescent to grossness, but it can also arouse a great desire for purity in him. My unblushing romanticism, much aided by a total lack of money and a ferocious shyness, persuaded me that I, poised upon peaks of passion never yet attained, was marked out for loves for which I had to keep myself free from any stain—Iseult, Beatrice, or Juliet.

But nature cannot be repressed as easily as all that. I could not manage to drive luscious imaginings away. Our maid's bosom, the plumpness of a female leg, the curve of a neck—these were so many torments. There were some objects that assumed an emotional power over me, a power that derived from the most far-fetched analogies. Women wore long kid gloves and high-buttoned boots in those days, and I was not the only person for whom these had an erotic significance; but I extended this fetishism to cover anything and everything that was made of leather. The sound of silk gripped me by the throat, whatever its source; a patch of lawn brought to my mind the thought that two might lie upon it. I still do not know whether it was an inherited weakness or an excessive degree of virility, but for many years I was awakened with extreme suddenness three or four times every night. In midwinter I slept with no more than a single sheet over me. Presently, by a merely mechanical effect, any sort of contact became perilous—the saddle of a bicycle or a reasonably hard chair; and if I happened to be in any sort of a crowd, I never escaped from it unscathed.

You will tell me that a great many adolescent boys go through much the same kind of crisis and emerge from it quite happily. I am not so sure. How many sexual perversions, unwholesome ways, strange quirks, maladjustments, and apparently causeless kinds of violence have as their origin just this sort of physical debilitation and moral disturbance? Up until the third form I had been a very bright pupil, and then all at once, although my written work was still tolerably good, I turned utterly stupid when confronted with a trifling verbal question. A complete blank—I could not even bring out a vaguely correct answer, nor yet an apology: not a single word. Yet I had scarcely sat down again, marked with a naught that stung like a brand of infamy, when my memory came back to me.

How did it happen that the master was not astonished at finding a dullard instead of the exceptionally bright boy he had been told to expect? The school had chosen me as its representative in some competition or other between the fifth-form pupils, and he could not have been unaware of it. So why did he not take me aside and try to restore my self-confidence? No doubt he did not consider it his business, in much the same way that a good many parents do not consider it theirs either.

Although I was quite popular at school, there was nevertheless something of a gap between me and the other boys, and this arose from my earliest schooling. I was the product of a French mother and a Dutch father, and my father's business—he was a diamond broker—obliged us to leave France when I was three, so that my education began in Amsterdam. My brother and I were provided with a Dutch governess, but we went on speaking French, and French alone, with our parents.

My father settled in Paris when he was twenty, ten years before his marriage, and he fell so much in love with France that he developed a very high degree of chauvinism. The slightest hostile criticism of his adopted country sent him into a furious rage. In a hasty generalization he defined his fellow countrymen in the following terms. "A Dutchman," said he, "is a fellow who comes to Paris on August 15, sits on the terrace of the Café de la Paix and gazes for hours at the other foreigners who have also come to see the capital, goes to see *Faust* at the Opéra, and then returns home observing that Frenchwomen do not deserve their reputation for style and good looks." He was therefore very anxious that his children should finish their schooling in France, and he was scarcely settled in Amsterdam before he was already planning to get back to Paris.

Our return to Paris in 1900 is still one of the clearest and most delightful of my childhood memories. Until they could take possession of the flat they had rented in the rue de Vienne, my parents took rooms in the Hôtel de Bade, which was on the Grands Boulevards, between the rue Taitbout and the rue du Helder. By the time the trunks were unpacked, it must have been ten o'clock; then we went downstairs to take a walk. It was the end of May: a warm evening. The flowers on the horse chestnuts in the boulevard were only just beginning to drop. The whole world seemed to me to be swimming in a supernatural blue light. Cabs went trotting by, and the cheerful sound of their horses' hoofs was punctuated by the tinkle of the bells on their harness. There were others crawling along for hire, and their drivers wore white leather top hats that fascinated me. Cafés, filled with customers, spilled out over the pavements. There was an unknown scent in the air—the smell of absinthe. I was rediscovering a paradise that had been buried in my heart, but I was not quite sure that I might not be dreaming, and (helped by the weariness of a long journey) in my happiness I could scarcely walk straight.

We "did" Paris as though we were tourists, that is to say, we saw it more thoroughly than any Parisian born ever sees it all his life. From the Terrasse des Feuillants in the Tuileries we saw the Place de la Concorde below us, more nobly proportioned than any other, and the whole run of the Champs-Élysées. All the length of the Cours-la-Reine and as far as one could see along the Seine, there was the Exposition (late, like every other exhibition since the first the world ever saw), with its foreign pavilions still being built, all taking the toy shop as their inspiration. Toward the Invalides, a rising mass of whipped cream gave a foretaste of the buildings intended to house the French exhibits. The only thing that was finished was Binet's monumental gate. Its huge arch, dotted with countless colored lights, opened onto the Cours-la-Reine; on the top of it there was the Parisienne welcoming the Universe, and on either side, two tall columns that Rémy de Gourmont happily described as fretted phalluses. The posing, affected Parisienne and the whole edifice, the finest flower of what was then the modern style, came in for some bitterly unkind criticism: today it would make us melt with tenderness.

We were sent directly to the little Lycée Condorcet, in the seventh form. At the first French dictation lesson my brother and I were at the top of the class. And that was where the trouble lay! We spoke as we wrote, somewhat too perfectly. We had not had those five or six years of slangy, incorrect, abbreviated talk with other schoolboys speaking the same language—we did not know the French equivalent of feins or bags I or oh, what a swizz. We asked astonishing questions. Seeing a priest who had come to fetch two young pupils, I asked, "Is he their father?" as though I were still living in a Protestant country. There was another thing that set us apart: we were Jews, and the hubbub caused by the Dreyfus affair was only just beginning to die down. Yet I must admit that I never felt the slightest enmity arising from this from my companions, nor did I hear any sort of sarcastic remark. For although in France anti-Semitism may sometimes have been violently expressed in the papers and in public, and although it formed part of certain political platforms and may form part again, there is no country in the world where it has less effect upon social relationships. In Holland, on the other hand, where Jews had always been freely admitted and where no law and no section of public opinion has ever molested them, the separation between the communities remained very firm. Furthermore, this was a reciprocal racist attitude: my very orthodox uncles did not merely not associate with Gentiles, but if they had, they would have kept them at a distance. In this way, the withdrawal came from us. My father never dreamed of inviting my school fellows to our house, and he would not have liked it if I had gone to theirs.

This want of perfect identity between my companions and myself was still in being when my puberty reached its height and accentuated my isolation. Could their opinions have provided me with salvation? I feel that it is by no means easy for any boy between thirteen and sixteen, whether he has money or not, to find an outlet for his passions. But at least I should have learned that I was not alone in my suffering and that it did not possess the abnormal and even monstrous character that I ascribed to it. Secrecy, anxiety, a turning in upon myself: nothing was more suited for keeping up the unhealthy state that was draining me of strength.

I still have a kind of incapacity for forming strong attachments with males of my own species, and I date it from this period. When I look back, I see that my real friendships have been with women. There is something that I cannot define that separates me from most men: it may be hunting, which I cordially dislike because of my love of animals; or fishing; or that air that they have, like bumblebees stuffing themselves into every flower; or the commercial traveler's jokes; or the belly laughs . . . Friendship implies a certain complicity.

Really I think it was my father's business, and his alone, to come to my help. What a difficult role it is to play, that of a father. There are precious few who find the right measure between Olympian grandeur and a disproportionate mateyness. Mine insisted upon forms of respect which no doubt had their origins in far-off Eastern countries and which I do not in any way criticize in themselves. At no time of my life did I ever meet my father in the street without taking off my hat and keeping it off until he told me to put it on again. He never traveled by train without my coming to see him off. It is true that he did as much for me—a fact that was not without its embarrassing side when I became a young man and stopped traveling alone. He was a medium-sized man with regular features, a trim mustache, and a fan-shaped beard. In all my days I never heard him utter a word of slang, not even the most harmless; and of course I was equally circumspect when I spoke in his presence.

My mother was small and dark, and rather than true beauty, she had the fine freshness of youth. She was intensely alive, a woman to her fingertips, and very good at music: she thought a great deal of dress and social success. For her own delight and as a sort of game, she also cultivated the domestic row. My father would let himself be trapped into her cruel game. Then anxious, trembling, we children would hear the rising storm and the flood of bitter words.

It was in scenes with the maids that my mother really outdid herself. She would come back from one of these with her face scarlet and her eyes glittering with excitement. "I gave her a piece of my mind," she would say in a triumphant voice. Poor wretched servants, who were at that time neither people with a proper set job nor yet members of the household, but who dwelt in fireless attics that could scarcely be called rooms, working from seven in the morning until midnight, with no thought of any holidays; and when they were dismissed they were obliged to undergo the additional humiliation of having their meager belongings searched. I remember that I was invariably on their side and against my mother.

To be sure, my mother loved us and took great care of us. She was nevertheless capable of being very untimely with her severities, and nothing wounds children more than that. One can very well put up with a box on the ears; but having to stand with one's arms down and face held up for the blow is not a punishment so much as an outrage. Sometimes, too, we were allowed little scenes of our own, cut down to our size; and I have the feeling that in these modest performances my mother was running through her scales by way of practice for higher things.

When I think of her, my mind is haunted by a kind of uneasiness. It is not that I did not always show her the utmost consideration: but I do blame myself for not having had that very strong feeling for her which speaks of the prime human relationship perfectly maintained. They are fortunate indeed, those for whom the gentle name of mother always retains its exquisite sound.

In short, all that was lacking in what was in many respects a model home was warmth and affection. All things being considered, I was fonder of my father; but I should never have dreamed of telling him of my bodily disturbances or my other uncertainties, and I believe he would have found any confidences of this kind most unwelcome. But surely there must be some way of keeping one's authority without necessarily repelling confidence. Of course, it would call for a degree of tact and intuition which does not, I suppose, ordinarily fall to the average run of mankind. If only all parents had a genius for their role!

What would my father's advice have been? Perhaps his character would have prevented him from treating the question of sex with me, but at least, in order to render me somewhat less obsessed, he might have insisted upon my taking exercise—the counterpoise of fresh air and healthy physical tiredness. Yet my parents were city dwellers and opposed to sport to an extent that can scarcely any longer be conceived of since the coming of the motorcar. My father would not allow us children or my mother to go into the Bois de Boulogne, on the grounds that the trees sucked all the oxygen out of the air for themselves. My mother looked upon life in the country as an incessant and pitiless struggle with snakes, scorpions, eagles. The sun was the great enemy, and no precautions were too arduous to preserve one from its strokes.

There were still the holidays. The first essential was to flee the heat. So for a month we were taken to Boulogne-sur-Mer, for Boulogne was both a town and a place where it might very well be cold. Here my parents made a great concession to that mania for sport that was reaching us from England—a mania that ran utterly counter to all natural good sense. Every morning we were entrusted to a fully clothed, hatted swimming instructor, whose method of teaching consisted in towing us for very long periods through the icy water by hand. When this delight was over we were slowly brought back to our senses by violent massaging, hot foot baths, and a glass of Malaga.

The clash between the generations turned out to be very pronounced in the case of my father and my brother: they had long-lasting disputes and arguments. My brother was thistledown where I was lead. Very early he started coming home late at night and getting up late, and he was somewhat given to lying. During these discussions I heard my name brought forward as an example. Now, in fact what I provided was rather an example of what not to do. I spent the whole of the time that was not taken up by my studies shut up in my bedroom reading, and I hardly ever went out. I turned in upon myself more and more. I passionately wanted to write, and I dare say I was as capable or as incapable as the average young man; but since my models were Dante and Shakespeare, I wanted to reach the sublime straightaway, and the sublime did not present itself to me on a plate.

I still have a photograph of myself taken at that time. I am sitting there in a Gothic armchair, half leaning toward an ancient folio open upon a table. My hair is carefully parted in the middle; my brows are knitted, and my gaze is fixed upon something far away. The intense expression on the whole face makes it quite clear that the person whose message the world awaits impatiently is being stirred by uncommonly deep thought.

I also thought that within myself I could detect a genius for the stage that would make the most famous actors turn pale with envy. And in this at least I did find an audience in the form of the woman who came in by the day to do sewing for my mother. Declaiming all the parts myself, I recited the entirety of Victor Hugo's plays to her. She paid such attention, without any of the features of her somewhat blotchy and wholly unmade-up face even stirring, that I now suspect her of never having listened at all. My most terrible harangues never lit the slightest spark behind those archaic pince-nez. As for me, the whir of the sewing machine, for want of any other applause, far from damping my enthusiasm, urged me on to fresh heights.

But this meek and accommodating audience did not provide me with an adequate safety valve. I had no contact with real life; I rejected friendship; I was physically exhausted; mentally I was getting nowhere; and I was gloomy, lonely, and in a fair way to becoming dangerously etiolated.

What would have happened to me if, when I was

about seventeen, I (a lesser Descartes) had not had my "night of illumination"? Reason, or at least resigned acceptance of the reasonable, came to me one day, as abruptly as a bump rising on my forehead. With a fresh, unflattering eye I reread my latest efforts and found them revolting. I asked at once for an interview with my father. I informed him that the work that I felt growing within me was of such dimensions that it needed time for ripening. Until it should have brought me fame and fortune, could he supply my needs? At the same time I did not conceal from him the fact that these needs were about to increase markedly, since I intended to leave my ivory tower and lead the life of a young man of my own age in order to provide myself with material and experience for my future novels.

In his turn, my father confessed to me that he was quite without fortune, that he was living from one day to the next, and that his means did not allow him the luxury of keeping a hothouse plant in his home. Nevertheless, I detected a note of disappointment in his voice. For some time past, he had been urging me to accept a commercial post, pointing out that the few poets who escaped dying of hunger ended their days in the poorhouse. I accomplished nothing by holding up Victor Hugo against his Verlaine. Still, I had to some degree succeeded in winning him over, and he did not wholly reject the flattering notion that he might have begotten a prodigy. In the sigh of relief that he heaved on seeing me return to the ranks of prudence and good sense, may there not have been some regret for a lost illusion?

As for me, I was in a furious hurry to bring about my total change of attitude. I went and stood naked in front of a looking glass, and my image gave me no pleasure at all. Narrow-shouldered, narrow-chested, pallid: I looked to myself like some kind of a turnip that had been blanched in a cellar. I immediately determined to cultivate this long-neglected body. Just as for years I had followed my own inclinations, so now I longed to force myself in the other direction, and I sought out the sport that would go most against my natural bent. I had never been very brave and at school I had always avoided fighting, being of the opinion that the puniest of my companions was stronger than I: so I now chose boxing.

At that time amateurs still boxed merely for the pleasure of boxing, without any ulterior motive, any idea of competition or professionalism—a state of affairs that hardly applies today. My first and hardest victory was walking through the door of a training establishment where young men were exchanging what appeared to me horrifying blows, to speak to the instructor and to make an appointment with him. A little later, then, I fould myself dressed in little but my emaciated nakedness, with boxing gloves on my fists, face to face with my destiny in the form of a stocky athlete named Bayle—by no means the same Bayle as the one my reading had made me familiar with. The first sharp and sounding punches that I delivered filled me with admiration for myself, for I did not realize that it was the instructor who was making his padded glove go bang against mine. A kind of well-being began to invade my person: O wonder! my muscles were doing what they were called upon to do, my legs were obeying me.

Showered, toweled, and dressed again, I found myself outside, and for the first time in my life I was aware of a kind of happiness from the mere fact of drawing breath. "To breathe in happiness" stopped being a figure of speech as far as I was concerned. As early as that very day, I began to suspect that happiness was in the first place essentially connected with respiration.

I had flung myself into boxing as I might have decided to drown myself, and I found by chance that I was particularly well suited to it. One never knows one's physical possibilities until one has tried them out. Had I gone on marking time in a kind of half-imprisonment, I should no doubt have come to the end of mine. But youth and elasticity are synonymous, and a few months of diligent exercise were enough to transform me. My first match brought me into the ring with a young fellow who looked far more muscular than I—the mere sight of him almost made my heart die within me.

My opponent rushed upon me at once. I warded off his blows as well as I could, and to prevent myself from being utterly destroyed, I attacked in my turn. As I had been taught, I shot out a straight left and followed it with a right hook to the jaw, a punch that was impelled by dread and that therefore had all my strength behind it. Miraculously, the youth sagged, fell into a clinch, and from then on did nothing but take avoiding action, cover himself, and cling. Without a moment's pause I passed from terror to overweening presumption and danced round my opponent, indulging myself in the pleasure of making him last. So I too could inspire fear, I who had suffered from it so much! My bosom swelled as I realized that I had won at such immensely long odds against myself. I was drunk with pride. I discovered in myself the astonishing treasures of speed, lithe ease, a cool head, and an exact sense of distance.

Going from one extreme to another, I put myself in training for years on end as though I had been a professional, and as often as I could, I fought against professionals. In the street the passers-by gazed in amazement at the young lunatic who rolled his shoulders as he walked, swinging quick little hooks into the empty air. Or sometimes I would suddenly hurry toward one of them and, at the very moment when it seemed that I must infallibly bang into him, make a little side step that left him standing, aghast.

I have always kept myself in training: in my young days I went about it with the utmost zeal; later on, with moderation. In rather too specialized a way, I think. I am sorry never to have known the delights of athletics or of winter sports. I have gone on frequenting the ring because that was how I began. When I was sixty-five I took to tennis, never having handled a racquet before. I am keeping golf in reserve for when I grow old.

What I like about the practice of a sport is not only the proper maintenance of the human machinery but just as much the momentary return to simplicity. Arguing for hours as to whether a given movement should be carried out with the shoulder below or otherwise seems to me a healthy occupation. With all general notions done away with, the mind is brought back to a single elementary technical question, and this is very restful to it. I am perfectly well aware that nowadays most young people do go in for sport, but there are still many who do not like it, and nearly all give it up too soon. To amass skills and then to let the mechanism that should make use of them clog up seems to me utterly mad.

My efforts at turning conformist were not limited to this. I, who by turns had dreamed of becoming—and that without making the slightest degrading compromise—a great poet, an inspired actor, a condottiere, a popular leader, a reformer, had no longer anything but one single ambition, that of turning into an average man. Not that I am now so very proud of so total an abdication. That I left my pedestal with such tameness no doubt proves that it was made of clay. I shall never throw a stone at any adolescent who to the bitter end refuses any fate other than that which he has chosen for himself, even though he may come to grief over it.

I had no time to lose for the sowing of my wild oats. To reach the heart of Paris by night, I had only to follow my brother: he knew every path and short cut. Full-blown Parisian life was still pretty brilliant, and at first I found it by no means devoid of attraction. It was founded upon a long tradition, that of the cult of woman worship. The brilliance of the last great courtesans was sending out its final blaze; and sometimes I saw them, perched on the high bar stools at Maxim's, their skirts spread out and low, their arms covered, necks invisible under whale-boned cloth, face half hidden by an immense picture hat. The more accessible they were, the harder of approach they seemed. They were wholly out of my reach, but everything about them aroused my stunned admiration, even their borrowed noble names: Émilienne d'Alençon, Liane de Pougy, Liane de Lancy . . .

In the Champs-Élysées the bar of the Palace and Fouquet's, and at Montmartre the Abbaye de Thélème, the Rat Mort, Palmyre's, Pigall's, and the night clubs on the rue Fontaine, acted as centers of attraction for a whirling band of young men on a spree, and for some who were not so young too. Most had their wenches with them; others trusted to chance pickups to finish what remained of the night. For they all behaved as though going home to bed was a punishment that had to be avoided at any cost. We knew the bar that closed the latest and the club that waited longest before giving warning and then finally turning out its lights. As a last resource, there were the Halles, the great central markets, with their illusion of low adventure—crumpled silk dresses brushing against the butchers' aprons with their new-spilt blood. In the summer, when dawn came up, we used to go to the farm of the Pré-Catelan. There, before the lackluster eyes of the lined-up cows, the new milk was served out, a purifying flood for drawn, debauched, and sunken faces.

Sitting on the pavement at Fouquet's, I saw many faces pass to and fro: there was Fréhel, the singer, tall, thin, scornful, smooth-complexioned, almond-eyed; the wings of her nose moved expressively, and there was a cigarette holder stuck in the corner of her mouth—Fréhel, with whom I fell hopelessly in love. And there was Gaby Morlay, tiny, high-cheeked, with a smile that wrinkled up her face, still at that time waiting to be a star; and Yves Mirande with his hat, his stick, and his eyebrows, his heart as adventurous as his stories. More rarely, there was Mistinguett, and when she appeared she was at once badgered by men she did not know, for there was no reputation that rivaled hers. The whole of show business was dominated by her tall, trembling white feathers.

Mistinguett acted as badly as she danced and sang. One tries to make out the nature of the glamour that made her irreplaceable for forty years, and one tries in vain. Colette used to put it down to an unparalleled physical harmony. Others spoke of an extraordinary personality, which explains nothing. Her success outlived the Great War and even the three-percent bonds, though she was thought to be an institution of the same kind, based upon immutability.

It seemed to me quite unimaginable that I should ever one day be familiarly acquainted with these well-known people. In me, as in all the young, the worship of idols was to be found next door to iconoclasm. Today it seems to me perfectly natural that I should have written a play in collaboration with Yves Mirande. During the German occupation, Gaby Morlay proved herself a perfect and immensely helpful friend, and her recent death grieved me bitterly. The candles that she lit, praying to Our Lady of Victories for my release from internment, still stand firmly in my heart. As for Mistinguett, I remember her with Colette and me at Saint-Tropez before it became so frantically overrun, sitting round a table at Sénéquier's, which has since become one of the world's top places. Miss, whose ambition was always the legitimate stage, begged Colette to write a play for her, as touching a play as possible. "I should so love to make them snivel," she wailed.

After a long disappearance, Fréhel returned to the stage in about 1935, and she won back the public's favor right away. At that time, together with Joseph and Georges Kessel, I was bringing out a weekly paper called *Confessions,* which had a brief career, and which deserved a better fate. Entrusted by my companions with writing up Fréhel's memories, I went to see her by appointment in a little café in the rue Chaptal. I knew that she had changed a great deal, but still it did a little something to my heart when I opened the door of the place and saw, sitting in front of a drink, a broad matronly figure with her features drowned in the puffy fat of her face and her hair devoid of life. She hailed me in a cheerful, vinous, common voice, and as soon as I sat down she began to tell me the story of her life, all in impulsive jerks. In Tsarist Russia the grand-dukes had flung jewels at her feet. Meanwhile I was trying, though furtively, to bring back to life the clean, sharp young being who had served as Colette's model for the character of Jadin in *La Vagabonde;* but like Chéri in *La Fin de*

Chéri, I could only repeat, "Where is she? Where is she?"

She fell silent, and to fill the pause, I spoke of past days, telling her how much in love with her I had been. A grin raised her dewlaps, a brief light appeared in her eyes, and from her worn mouth there dropped the dismaying words, "It is never too late to do good." I stammered out a few civil words. It is not military retreats alone that have their difficulties.

My brother brought me into a group of young men of our own age, and here again I stood out, a lonely figure. Among the girls who moved around our set there were some I liked well enough, though not with the "big emotion" I was waiting for. The one I liked most was called Jacqueline. She was a dark girl with a rather mat complexion, and her face still had something of its childish ingenuity; her way of moving reminded me of Fréhel. But I should never have dreamed of setting up as a rival to her friend René, a very good-looking young man of about twenty and one to whom she seemed faithful. I was with them at the bar of the Café de la Paix one evening, and René had to leave us because of some social engagement. He had scarcely gone when Jacqueline informed me in the most straightforward manner that it was not René she loved, but me. She handled this declaration of love like a bludgeon.

Discovering that I was beloved for myself alone by one of the prettiest girls I knew made me blaze up like powder. But as soon as there was a pause in my lyrical outpourings, Jacqueline cut me short, saying, "I'm tired. What about going home to bed?" I was somewhat taken aback by this observation, which seemed to verge on the primitive, and it occurred to me that perhaps the first fruits of a great love might be different from what I had imagined them to be: I accompanied my new "girl friend" to her tiny flat in Montmartre. There I took her in my arms, but she disentangled herself, saying that she felt the coming of a sty and that she had to look after it at once. After a long, long time, she came out of the bathroom with one eye covered by a broad black bandage that hid half the other as well; so that it was with Justice personified that I had my first tender passage of arms, or so it seemed to me—all the more so since Justice Jacqueline not only looked her part but also provided the traditional frigidity.

I opened my eyes in the morning; I could not make out whether Nemesis had done the same, but I was getting ready to utter the crow of a contented cock when a maid came in bearing a missive that she handed to Jacqueline. Jacqueline's bandage rose at last. "That's for you," she said, passing me the mysterious paper, which was nothing other than her landlord's bill. "It's rent day today and I'm broke."

In my pocket there was a sum equivalent to the monthly pay of the job I then had: without a word I offered it up on the altar of a love whose flames thereupon went out. This single stroke taught me to suspect the motives of others, and even to wonder about René's sudden departure the evening before; like a flag in a dead calm, my illusions drooped; with a heavy step and a vile taste in my mouth, furnished from now on with experience that was never to be any use to me, I walked slowly home, where, to cap all, I was received with a series of gloomy warnings from my father.

I grew tired of "life" as soon as I became aware of its everyday, routine character. Many people set about their gaiety in the same bureaucratic state of mind that they would have adopted for the civil service, traveling the same round every night, scarcely varying by so much as a minute. Tigre, the son of the writers Henri de Régnier and Gérard d'Houville,[1] is still the stock example. "Spring," said he, "begins with the opening of the racing season at Longchamp." He

[1] Madame de Régnier's pen name.

might have added, "And day at five o'clock." It was then that he got up: his barber was ready for him, and the shaving was accompanied by great draughts of red wine—a first sign of returning life. Tigre de Régnier was endowed with an unconquerable beard that blackened his face from as early as two in the morning, when he was only a third of the way through his night. His reason for living ended by turning into the living itself, his trade; for the weekly *Gringoire* took him on as its night-club reporter, and never was there a more conscientious journalist. He died as he had lived, succumbing to a barely excessive dose of one of those dangerously sophisticated spirits that were sold for their weight in gold during the last—or, shall we say, the most recent—war.

We were then gently traveling along toward our particular war, without having any notion of the fact. For a long time we had been used to seeing the great nations scowling at one another (Agadir and Fashoda, and that sort of thing), and we were comforted by the famous European balance of power, which in fact was nothing but a tottering pile of gunpowder barrels: suddenly the very active and living ogre appeared in front of us. I believe that I was not the only one to receive him with a half-hidden, or perhaps I should say unavowable, satisfaction. Fate was plucking me out of a blind alley, and I might never have emerged without its help.

I had just passed my twenty-fifth birthday. In the end I had followed in my father's footsteps and I had a place in the pearl and gem-stone trade that anyone might have envied. My health was good; I cannot have been actually repulsive to look at; I had more spending money than I knew what to do with. Like a little marquis out of Molière, I might have stood in front of a looking glass and have stated that I was thoroughly satisfied with myself. In fact, I was bored to the pitch of extinction. I was paying the price of my submission. How many of us are there who have within us neither a demon strong enough to thrust us on into adventure nor yet a good angel wise enough to keep us to the beaten track; and who drag a nostalgia for our boyhood dreams throughout our lives?

I had refused to compromise on one point only: no sooner had I formed an amorous connection than I began to think of breaking it. This was not fickleness, but rather a faithfulness to my former lofty notions of what a loving pair should be.

Generally speaking, in order not to run the risk of growing attached to them, I preferred what might be termed fancy tarts to women I met socially or to affectionate and sometimes disinterested girl friends. So it happened that I would display myself in fashionable restaurants, where on given days I had my table reserved for me, in the company of creatures whose only merit was a certain knack of wearing the ermine stole that I gave them, paying for it by installments. I left them, and the monthly payments went running on: so did I. When I think of myself putting on a dinner jacket almost every evening, with a monocle screwed into my eye, unwarrantably familiar with headwaiters, dictatorial, overlavish with tips, it seems to me that I must have been the very type of the *petit crevé*, the fop with a strong dash of the bounder. The worst of it was that the character I was playing did not amuse me. You would have said that I was taking my revenge on someone, or some thing, or on myself. Like the journalist Arthur Meyer, who thrust aside his opponent's sword with his left hand in a duel, I too might have murmured, "Only a war can cause this to be forgotten."

To be sure, I had no illusions about this war. I did not see it as any kind of a heroic cavalcade, and I knew what kind of misery it was going to cause. I would have given everything I possessed in the world to prevent its taking place. But once there was nothing I could do about it, I was by no means displeased in my heart of hearts (that is what one calls the place where one's perverseness dwells) that the monotony of my life should be roughly disrupted, even if there had to be a disaster to do it.

Now that I have just run through my childhood and youth, I find that even I had not supposed they were so devoid of happenings, so bare of moving recollections. That is true, moreover, only because I see them again in the same way that I saw them then. Those particular days are not so much to be blamed as the person who judged them. Youth is too rich to stop to count its wealth; and it is no part of its nature to take notice of happiness. Today I dream of writing a book about a single day in which nothing whatever should happen but of which every moment should be valued at its true worth and fully savored.

My purpose here is not—and I should be very sorry indeed if I were misunderstood—is not to accuse the young in a sly, underhand way on the pretext that my present condition, my present age, seems to me the most delightful of all. At the utmost I might feel tempted to pity them, if I were not aware that my pity would only meet theirs halfway. However one embarks upon it, it seems to me that the dialogue between them and me must be difficult. They will call that gentleness which makes me no longer hate or despise anything mere apathy; this harmonious inner agreement with myself, stagnation; this acquiescence in life, in its ills as well as its joys, senile resignation. Although the line *The grapes are green, says he* may never cross their lips, I can see it dancing in their eyes. And I, if I were to let myself go and shout at them, "But I am the one who has got hold of the right end!" —could I prevent myself from inwardly murmuring, "Yes, but it *is* the end"?

In a most entertaining book called *1914*, the German publicist Emil Ludwig puts forward the view that no one really wanted the First World War and that events very rapidly acquired a momentum of their own against which those in power struggled in vain. He speaks of a whole train of minute cogs in this fatal series—an important meeting between two diplomats, for example, that was canceled because the new dress of one of the wives had not been sent in time. Very well. I have no objection to anybody's advancing the bad luck that allowed matches and other objects carefully chosen for their liability to burst into flames to lie about in a powder magazine. If you want war, prepare for war. If you want peace, do not put your trust in a complex of military alliances, a cardhouse balance of power, displays of fighting strength, and music-hall rhetoric. Otherwise a moment will come when it seems easier to cut the Gordian knot rather than untie it. Wars, like private murders, are often merely outbursts of diffidence.

It was because of one of these outbursts of diffidence that one day I found myself at dawn in a railway truck intended for the reception of forty men or eight horses; and at that moment men were more urgently needed.

On reaching twenty-one, I had opted in favor of Dutch nationality in order to escape military service, for which I had but an indifferent appetite. Yet war was another matter altogether. I belonged to France with all my being; I was attached to her by her skies, her cathedrals, her history, her virtues, her faults, and the lovely ring of her name. Any attack upon her was an attack upon me. The call to arms, coming from the remotest depths of time, awoke an immediate response in me. Taking part and going through it with the rest was not so much a temptation to me as an overruling necessity. So I should have needed more courage to stay comfortably at home than to enlist.

Yet enlisting was not as easy as one might have supposed. Day after day I went to the Invalides, where
there was a recruiting center meant for the reception
of foreign volunteers but which did not seem to have
much idea of what to do with them. "They will see to
you presently." Meanwhile, the volunteers naturally
fell into groups according to their nationality, and I
joined the Belgian-Dutch contingent. So as not to lose
a single hour of preparation, we trained ourselves in a
cellar with sticks, under the orders of an utterly delighted former Belgian captain, who could not have
served since the Belgian war of independence. Finally
we were told that we could not be drafted into French
units since as foreigners we were unable to speak
French; and so we were to be sent to swell the ranks of
the Foreign Legion. As we were almost all Parisians of
long date, our first difficulty, once we were in the
army, was to understand the instructors they gave us.
I remember a Danish captain whose desires we never
could make out: I remember no more than one of his
orders, given on a day when he was making a particular effort to be comprehensible. "At the first whis-
tlings, everybody down the drain!"

Our marching orders came through. A long goods
train was waiting for us at the Gare d'Austerlitz, and

we piled in, a thousand men in a high state of patriotic excitement. After a very, very long wait, the train began to move. We traveled at nearly sixteen miles an hour. At every stop—and there were many of them—people hurried to see these strange creatures, still in mufti, who were wildly singing soldiers' songs. "Where are you going?" they cried. "To the frontier," we shouted back as one man. Yes, but it was the Spanish frontier. For it was at Bayonne, to be precise, that the First Regiment of the Foreign Legion underwent its military training, and it did not leave for the front until October 23, 1914.

There was some degree of turmoil in the trucks filled with the Belgians and Dutch. Our group was under a self-elected committee which included a chairman, a vice-chairman, a secretary-general, and several deputies. Each one of them claimed the honor of introducing us in due form to the French civil and military authorities who would of course receive us at our journey's end with tears in their eyes, and each had prepared a speech. "I am the one to do the talking!" cried the chairman. "I am the senior member," cried another.

During one of the stops, part of the committee got out to have a drink in the station bar. Suddenly the train set off without them. Sixty miles farther on, they joined us again, having managed to hire a car, and they accused their fellow members of having caused the train to make its treacherous start so that they alone should have the glory of addressing the generals, prefects, mayors, and other French bigwigs at the terminus. The main quarrel and its side issues were still going on at nightfall, when we stopped a little past Bayonne and got out.

The only person waiting for us was a solitary sergeant of the Legion with a battered kepi, a leary eye, and a voluminous mustache. A little taken aback, but not much, the chairman drew his speech from his pocket and began, "Gentlemen . . ."

"Now then, now then, you people who have joined up for a square meal," cried the sergeant in a gravelly voice, looking scornful at our crumpled, motley band. "Get yourselves into fours if you can manage it, and by the right, quick march!" A dismal silence hung over our ranks as we plodded toward the barn where we were to stay throughout our training—committee, subcommittee, and plain members, all lying in the same egalitarian straw.

Sitting on our kitbags, abruptly reminded of the fact that war does not consist solely of heroic song under shellbursts, we were sadly emptying the bottom of our knapsacks and water bottles when the sergeant, whose name was Franck (a German) and who seemed to be the only person there to look after us, burst violently in, bawling, "What's all this? Do I see wine? Don't you know it's forbidden? Here, you, give us a glass."

When his thirst was quenched, he disappeared, with final commands that sounded none the more dulcet for the quantities of wine he had drunk. "Remember this, you bunch of bums! Smoking is strictly forbidden. And you are not to forget to spit on your fag ends before you go to sleep."

We were making our entry into a world that possessed its own kind of logic and its own laws.

As for Sergeant Franck, he entertained so ferocious a dislike for his fellow countrymen that at first we were suspicious of him. And yet . . . On May 9, 1915, the First Regiment of the Foreign Legion, stationed in the Arras section, went over the top for the first time, in an utterly mad fashion, but one which would have been called "top hole" in the slang of the time. Just as in the days of Père Bugeaud, the buglers raced fifty yards ahead of the men and blew the charge until the last of them fell. Coming behind them, hunched forward, we ran across the turned-up ground so fast that we went through our own artillery barrage. I overtook and passed Sergeant Franck. He was a crack shot and he stood there, not taking the slightest precaution but rather drawing himself up tall, carefully aiming, firing, and advancing a few steps before starting all over again, giving and seeking death. A bullet hit him in the middle of the forehead.

How I should have loved to know his story! But he was far too secretive for anyone to be able to question him. Such a degree of hatred! Dark tragedy: darker crimes, perhaps.

After three miles of furious charging, we had thrust through all the enemy's defenses, but there were only a few of us left. We looked back: there was nothing to be seen. It may be that the gap was not wide enough to be exploited. However that may be, the reserves were close on twenty miles to the rear. Our feeling was rather that the officer in command of the operation had not believed that it would succeed. His name was Colonel Pétain.

On the other hand, the general who planned the attacks in the Champagne Pouilleuse in September 1915 believed in it only too heartily. For this operation the Foreign Legion was attached to the division under General Marchand, the man whom Fashoda had made famous. At that time all offensives had much the same look. It was the notorious "chewing away," which cost us so many teeth. After a violent artillery preparation, there was a charge; a few trenches were seized along a certain length of front, and then one was pinned down. We ended up blocked by a slope that also acted as a fairly good shelter from the Germans' fire.

I was musing on the way the Germans had commanded our positions from this height when I thought I saw something completely unreal: fifteen hundred yards behind us, the cavalry was trying to make its way out of a grove of trees. In comparison with this madness, the charge at Reichshoffen seems the most prudent action in military history. Quite apart from any activity on the part of the enemy, one has but to picture the ground peppered with shell holes, crisscrossed with barbed wire—an impossible terrain. I saw men falling, dismounted horses wheeling about. After a while, to my great relief, the cavalry turned back.

I dare say that according to the army manuals that were then in use the maneuver was correct: the cavalry should exploit any breach made by the infantry and pursue the enemy. The fact that our breach amounted to an advance of no more than a few hundred yards, and the enemy's retreat to a slight falling back upon a system of defense in depth, altered nothing: theory is theory.

I hope that there are still some other witnesses of this heroic stupidity or that it is written down somewhere: there was no reason at all why I should have seen visions that day, and my imagination is too feeble to have invented such a spectacle.

The trenches, the battles of Arras and Alsace, the Champagne offensive, a wound, convalescence, attachment to the British army, the armistice . . . The 1914 war has been the subject of too many books for me to linger over it. Four years out of the prime of my youth, out of the very flesh of the fruit. And yet I do not look upon them with too gloomy an eye. Perhaps because I cannot see what would have taken their place. For a tormented mind the absence of responsibility, at least as far as one's own self is concerned, is always a temptation. A kind of lyrical feeling never left me, a contrast with the conditions that surrounded me. I wrote verse with my feet in the mud, and from the front I brought back a little book of poems that I am not ashamed of. So I have to make an effort to bring back the long, dreary, shivering days in the trenches, with mud and dampness clinging, time that would not move on, the nights on guard with one's eyes staring, the perpetual millstones of boredom through which one passed again and again and again, the fear . . . yes, the fear. Yet what still comes spontaneously rising in my heart from time to time is some odd moment of happiness, some absurd shared laughter of those days, the almost stealthy feeling of human warmth, or the first green flush on an April wood.

In short, one's memory scarcely allows anything through its sieve other than those aspects of the past that can do one good. It draws the past off its lees and refines it. There remains to me now, of my life with Colette, whose death I thought would kill me, a strewing of radiant memories that are henceforward safe, out of harm's way, sacrosanct, a place in which my overburdened heart may unbosom itself, a presence, a diffused light that enriches my current life without encroaching upon it.

The news of the armistice reached me, as it reached everybody else, one gray November morning; but few heard it in drearier circumstances. At that time I was attached to the British army as an interpreter, and we had been chasing the retreating Germans for the last two days without the slightest desire to catch up with them. I had set out on horseback very early in the morning with two English officers, ahead of the troops, into a no man's land that stretched for a good seven miles, in order to see to the billeting of the men.

We had reached a little evacuated town just across the Belgian frontier. It was filled with the sadness of abandoned places, it had the same gaping look; and all this was made the worse by signs of recent life. Towards ten o'clock a motorcyclist appeared with orders. Among the instructions concerning victualing and daily military routine there lurked a couple of lines that stated, "Hostilities will cease on November 11 at 11.00 hours." The two Englishmen and I looked at each other in silence. None of us was in his own country and there was nothing to drink for miles and miles around. It was cold and all sound was muffled by the steady drizzle. The work we had to do was still as urgent as it had been before, and we were still at it at the moment when Paris and the other capitals exploded with joy, with little boys swinging on the gun carriages, and the prettiest girls on the soldiers' necks.

Did I really come back much changed from my contact with the most varied specimens of the human race at a time when they showed in their truest light, from my four years of confrontation with myself, years filled with "moments of truth"? I returned to a way of life that was practically the same as that which I had left. Like all demobilized soldiers, I had to readapt myself to it. "It's an ill wind that blows nobody any good," says an English proverb. The survivors of a war—and all wars are monstrous imbecilities—come out of it momentarily purified. Because they have been away from it long enough, the trivial round of everyday life, with its lies, its little compromises and cowardices, and its sly oppression of the weak, suddenly shocks them. Of necessity they have acquired an altruism that they find utterly wanting behind the front. They have seen a huge amount of suffering and they have dreamed of a better world; and now it seems to them that all this blood and all these tears have been shed in vain.

The authorities were not unaware of the amount of subversion that the demobilized brought back with them. The slowness of the demobilization (I was not allowed home until February 1919) had other motives as well, but that was at least one of them. As long as they arrived by dribs and drabs, society could manage to digest these apprentices in virtue and put them back on to the straight path of ordinary life. There would be a few general outbursts, a few allegedly inexplicable individual outbreaks of violence, and then presently everything would be calm.

The brotherhood of arms is not an empty phrase (except that there should no longer be any arms), but it withers fast when the climate changes. I do not think I shall surprise any ex-servicemen when I say that for quite a time I was sorry to have lost this comradeship. That man, upright as an oak—he was a chaplain—who carried me on his back when I was wounded, carried me across nearly a mile of churned-up earth . . . And that other fellow, whose arms and neck were shattered by grenade splinters and for whom all night long I lit one cigarette after another, putting them to his mouth and taking them away, so that between us we formed one single smoker . . . The water bottle whose last drop one gave away: the kit one carried for a weakening comrade . . . Lieutenant Doumic, who was the brother or the cousin of René Doumic and who had volunteered at an age that would have excused him from any service whatever: we had scarcely reached the front when he was killed, and four of us carried him in a tent canvas to the graveyard at Sillery; and you have to have done it to know what even a light corpse can weigh in those conditions . . .

The echoes of so different a world did not die away all at once. On September 28, 1915, the Champagne offensive was still raging. I was on liaison duties and I had just brought my platoon commander an order to advance from the wood in which we were lying flat on our bellies and reach another little wood about a hundred yards ahead, on the other side of a clearing that was swept by machine-gun fire. That very morning we had had added to our numbers a brand-new lieutenant who had just come up from the depot; he had never been near the front and he was out of his depth. Seeing that he was getting ready to line up his men and launch them into the open all together, I said to him, although I was only a private, "Leave it to me, sir. I'll look after it." I felt his relief. Along the edge of the wood I had detected a place where the men, so long as they went singly, might take advantage of the slope and have at least a chance of not being hit during their crossing. So I made them go one after the other, showing them the lay of the land—the places where it was possible to run doubled up and the places where they had to crawl. It all went smoothly. I set off last and I had scarcely gone a few yards when I was shot in the leg.

Two years after the armistice I was walking along the boulevard des Italiens and I heard someone calling me. "Goudeket! Goudeket!" I turned and recognized a man named Philips, one of those I had guided that September day. "You know those two fellows—" he said, without any preliminaries, "you said that as I went by I was to tell them it was no use lying there like that and they had to go as far as the wood?"

"Yes, I remember perfectly well."

"Well, old cock, do you know what? You know what? They were dead."

Philips was not an uneducated man: not at all, he was of quite a wealthy background. He was married and the cares that harass all young couples were harassing him; yet he nevertheless fell into the age-old trap of comradeship between men, even if only for the moment. Nothing seemed more important to him than to give an account of the mission I had entrusted him with five years before. And at the thought of the two dead men we had tried to persuade, we both burst out laughing.

I was obliged to acknowledge to myself that I had retained my basic inability to form links of either love or friendship. But I did come back from the war better armed against myself. Just as one's body manufactures its own counterpoisons, so my mind, delivered up to the unspeakable boredom of life in the trenches, had learned how to make use of a negative happiness that escaped from its surroundings.

Generally speaking, the need to understand the deep meaning of his own actions torments the adolescent only for a little while. He is either provided with what he finds a satisfactory answer by one of the religions or else he manages to thrust the problem aside, taking shelter in an unquestioning materialism. But I found that I was still haunted by the question *why*.

"Why this perpetual stirring of the universe, from the twirling atoms and the battles between the microbes right up to the conjunction of the stars? To what good purpose, to what end? Why this, why that, why me myself?"

Sometimes I thought I could solve it all with the formula: "God is the concept in which the question why does not have to be asked." All that remained was to reach God; and that I could not manage.

It was during one night in the war, when we were making earthworks in the Rheims sector, that I suddenly decided to take up a more delicate instrument than the flaming sword I had meant to wield until that moment. I abandoned the idea of finding any solution and I looked for some principle within my immediate grasp that might at least serve as a rule that would, definitively accepted, provide me with peace of mind.

Everything on this earth does its utmost, however blindly, to live a many-sided life. Everything that lives, breathes, flowers, does so all the time to the full extent of its abilities, and it struggles to the utmost limit of its strength before giving in. In the trenches the besoms that we made from twigs broke out into green buds in the spring. If the wind brings a trifle of earth to lodge in the most arid rock, presently a plant springs up. The microbes and viruses, attacked by poisons that almost annihilate them, work out mutations and become immune. Only man has that kind of intelligence—and it is probably no more than a manner of failure, decay—which allows him to argue about his very basis, to bring the whole matter into question and to attempt its destruction.

That was the point where one had to begin—one had to acknowledge that living, the obligation to live, was every sentient being's first law. It followed that a tepid approach to life was a violation of the law, and that preserving life was obedience to it. And since it is quite certain that happiness is favorable to life, making it more likely to last and to hand itself on, then happiness becomes the most imperative of duties.

Does there exist a more dreaded word? It is scarcely uttered when all the tribes and nations of the world fling themselves upon their amulets and fetishes, whisper protective formulas, and make propitiating signs in the air. Let no one tell me that all this is solely out of a fear of bringing bad luck. It is not only the term that is in question. I was there when Philippe Berthelot was asked for a few words for the late League of Nations' visitors' book, and paraphrasing Jules Romains he replied, "Peace is a precarious state that augurs no sort of good." That is what every man inwardly thinks of happiness. And so he plunges into the water to get out of the rain . . . or starts a preventive war.

But happiness as I mean it should be confused neither with hedonism nor with the cult of well-being that is based upon refrigerators, vacuum cleaners, and electric mixers. Nor even with the delight one feels at a fortunate happening, nor yet with that which comes to us from those we love, whatever kind of love it may be. Happiness is too precious a commodity to be left to mere contingency. It is a diffused, gratuitous joy that, being with us at each moment of our life, should become an integral part of it solely by the fact of our breathing.

A few years ago Orson Welles, that passionate, stentorian sybarite, discovered a little restaurant somewhere in the South of France—at Nice, I think it was —whose owner, between two games of *pétanque*, produced a series of Provençal dishes all of his own, so delightfully scented that they might have brought the dead back to life. Dazzled, and cherishing the eternal illusion that what is essentially local can be transplanted, Orson Welles conceived the notion of whisking this worthy soul, together with his immediate surroundings, his open shirt, his battered old slippers, his bowls, and his fine flow of speech, through the air as far as Hollywood, there to set himself up and found a dynasty. But the man remained unmoved by Welles's siren song, indifferent to the dazzling and daily increasing number of dollars proposed, and finally he answered in his broadest southern accent, "And what will you give me, God forbid, for my happiness?"

For indeed there is a *pétanque* player's happiness that is not wholly to be despised; but still it is a small, short-term kind of happiness. It depends on a blazing sun that thrusts through the shade of the plane trees on the haphazard pitch, on the dull thump of the bowls on the dusty earth, the mock rage of those who throw the bowl full-toss and those who drool it along the ground; it is based on wild southern exaggeration, siestas, garlic, rosemary, sweet basil, and Provençal rice, and it cannot even stand up against rain, let alone adversity.

Since respiratory happiness, the happiness one breathes in, derives from a fundamental agreement, from an oath that one has made to oneself, from an obligation that cannot possibly be broken, the search for it grows only the more imperative in times of adversity, sorrow, and misfortune.

Furthermore, a deep respect for life brings with it the duty of helping the lives of others and consequently of always remaining as adequate as possible.

Even our dead have need of us. I am not talking about their immortality, which is no business of ours, but about their survival on this earth. Our duty towards them is not finished by the mere shedding of tears. When they were living, they calculated the chances of this continuing existence, these lingering overtones, and it was upon us that they counted, for they knew that they would not really vanish until all recollection of them, even the memory of their names, had quite gone. So we owe them our life; and allowing it to be hurt, damaged, even under the weight of the sorrow we feel for their loss, is to betray them.

I take the most moving situation that I can imagine: a mother and father at the bedside of a child who is in danger of death. They are naturally, rightly, consumed with anxiety; and this anxiety is wholly bad for the child. But if I were to ask them to force themselves to cheer up, because that in itself amounts to a source of strength, a lever, and because we are quite ignorant of the way waves and fluids in one person may work upon another, why then, even if they did not happen to think my request monstrous, they would not be able to manage it. Oh, if only that winged breathing had become second nature to them! If the statesman at grips with a tragic decision, if the captain on the point of giving orders for a massacre, if only all men on earth . . . who can tell, who can tell?

I would not urge others to adopt my views if I had not tried them out upon myself. One must not expect to acquire this euphoria from one day to the next. Training and exercises are necessary. Begin by getting used to breathing deeply: your general state of health cannot but be improved by it. At each inward breath, say to yourself, "I am breathing, so I am happy," or else, "I am breathing, so it is my duty to be happy," or any other formula that you think will hasten the desired automatism in yourself. When you have reached it, the expression "walking on air" will no longer be a figure of speech for you. With your broadened chest you will indeed feel that there is a layer of air that is holding you up. Your reward, if you expect one, will be a truer appreciation of things, a soaring above all paltriness, a greater inner harmony. But above all you will observe that by a sort of contagion others who come into contact with you will have a feeling of happiness and comfort—you will have become beneficent.

When the Germans arrested me at dawn in December 1941, and when I was taken with a thousand other Jews to the camp at Compiègne after farewells that were all the more heartbreaking since both Colette and I tried to reassure one another and even to smile,

I at once saw that henceforward my best possible way of proving to Colette that I loved her was to survive, and that in order to do so I had to begin by abolishing, at whatever cost, the torturing image of our parting and live the life of the camp as though I had never known any other. Before leaving for Compiègne, we were herded together in the riding school of the École Militaire. Whether it was intention or mere chance I do not know, but we nearly all belonged to the same social group. René Blum (Léon's brother), Jean-Jacques Bernard, and Arnyvelde were there. Our gathering, under the wicked eye of a machine gun trained on us from a gallery, presently took on the air of a social occasion. "My dear fellow, what a long time since I had the pleasure of seeing you!" In such circumstances, social poise and respect for appearances are not without value: they provide a kind of first aid.

You think you know people; and then in emergencies they often behave in a totally unexpected manner. Arnyvelde was the youngest author ever to have had his plays acted at the Comédie Française; the fame of this remained, but it was gradually dying away as he busied himself with commonplace journalism. He attached himself to me at the camp, and together we often strolled up and down for hours in the prison compound. And for hours and hours Arny-velde complained: "They had absolutely no right whatsoever to arrest us."

"That's not the point," I replied.

"To arrest me—I served in the '14 war."

"That's not the point."

"If only I had gone into exile, as I had meant to at first!"

"Yes; but you did not."

He also told me about a mistress to whom he seemed much attached, and he continually harrowed his heart thinking about her. It was in vain that I tried to show him that if he went on lessening his re-sistance in this way he would presently find himself in the gravest danger. The first comparatively harmless malady would come upon him in this state of nervous collapse and carry him off in a few days.

The most senior member of our room, on the other hand, was a man called Bernheim; he was a very wealthy, very well known real-estate dealer, and he had led the most sheltered kind of life. We did not look upon him with much favor, possibly because the word "dealer" has quite unfairly retained a rather dis-agreeable ring. Yet from the very first day Bernheim got up before sunrise, made something that more or less resembled a broom, and set about cleaning the room with the utmost zeal. Then he washed, shaved, and dressed with great care. He volunteered for all fatigues, and we never heard him utter a single faint-hearted word. He was an example for many of us who might otherwise have given up hope.

Holding other peoples' heads out of the water is a capital way of preventing oneself from sinking, and I too set myself to it, as well as I could. But I was obliged to cut down on my winged breathing because it sharpens one's appetite. Very soon hunger became a torture. It has an obsessional quality that is degrading. Soon we were incapable of imagining that one could ever conceivably have refused a second helping or have eaten an orange without its peel as well or a herring without its head. I had recognized a friend in the Russians' camp: they were far better fed than we and they could also be sent parcels, whereas, because of reprisals for some assassination that I have forgotten about, we had no right to have anything sent to us. Every day, for hours on end, I waited for him at the end of the alley that separated the two camps, an alley dominated by a tower with a machine gun on it; my friend appeared and over the barbed wire he threw me a piece of bread that I carried off in my bosom. Looking back, I am far from ashamed of my begging: not at all—I am surprised and pleased that my instinct for self-preservation should have sprung up in full strength at the first call I made upon it. Scales of values and decorum vary according to the circles in which they are practiced. On the sinking *Titanic* a life belt was worth all the gold on earth. And at Compiègne Bernheim carried out the work of a saint.

Presently I found myself back in the daily round. I was thirty; I was quite well-to-do; I became the prey of well-intentioned matchmakers. It was time for me to join myself to some well-endowed girl, to have children by her, to grow acquainted with the domestic joys, and to claim a flattering place in the ranks of the bourgeoisie. I could find nothing better against these arguments than a stupid refusal. If I looked back at it with a candid eye, my past life had been nothing but a series of evasions; but for all that, I was still convinced that the long period of sentimental guard duty I had set myself would not prove to have been in vain.

One evening very like any other evening, I met Colette for the first time and for a moment my heart stopped beating. It was not a matter of her appearance—that of a handsome animal—or of her so very markedly individual face, or yet her outstanding personality. No: what I felt was the emotion of a man suddenly brought face to face with his destiny, who knows it, and who feels himself called upon to carry it through.

I may utterly have forgotten my childish words to my parents—uttered at a time when I scorned all reading other than the hopelessly abstruse—when I happened by chance upon a page of Colette: I then derived from her full-bodied prose a delight so near to physical pleasure that for years I told them that I would marry no other woman. But I instantly knew, without the shadow of a doubt, that I was now at my personal crossroads. My stubborn refusal to engage myself and my long waiting were now to show that they had a meaning, or that they were a failure.

As I exchanged my first words with Colette, who was sitting next to me at the table and whose strong Burgundian accent bowled me over, I became aware that, whatever happened, my life was about to change radically. I, a person wholly given up to literature, systems, rigid logic, and speculation, was coming into contact with the one being in the world who was more remote from them than any other. Everything she said showed that she was in the closest possible touch with all the things of everyday life; and she made their poetry apparent by the simple fact of naming them. In a simple-minded way, I decided that from then on the quest for naturalness should be my single aim. The person who filled me with this resolution spent thirty years in proving to me by the force of example that naturalness is an inherent quality and is not one that can be cultivated.

I have told the story of our life together in *Close to Colette*. It was a book that I began to write a year after Colette's death without really having thought how I should set about it. For four months, between eleven at night and three in the morning, in the total peace of the Palais-Royal, in the very place in which we had lived, in which not a single one of the objects that formerly surrounded us had been moved, I tried every night, in the yellow glow of my lamp, to bring our dead hours back to life. It seemed to me that sometimes another hand guided mine. Those were literally enchanted nights, in a silence that was no longer a loneliness. If the book did, as I hope it did, reflect the emotion that begot it, then it owes it all to those nights; and I thought that the portrait I was able to draw of Colette was finished for good and all.

I shall not add much to it, to be sure, except for what firmer lines time has been able to give. Perspective substitutes for the shifting truth of living features a certain unity that at first was by no means so clear. But, above all, the center of gravity of our thirty years together has changed for me. When I was writing *Près de Colette,* I was still wholly taken up with those last years we had passed without leaving one another for a single day, and I only touched slightly upon the early beginnings of our relationship, those shining hours at Saint-Tropez. It is those days that break in upon my memory now; and it is upon them alone that I shall dwell.

I have told how I met Colette in April 1925 in the house of mutual friends at Cap d'Ail, and how she drove back with me to Paris. Our attachment sprang up during this journey: our bond was not forged at once. To thank me, Colette invited me to luncheon in the little house she lived in by herself—69, boulevard Suchet, at Auteuil. The dining room and the drawing room seemed to me cold. It was clear that these surroundings were not of her choice. But these rooms gave on to a little garden in which Colette's own personal jumble of plants had their refuge—roses, heliotropes, rhododendrons, a hanging wistaria, to say nothing of the bush of aromatic herbs grown specially to welcome the visitor.

While the butler was there—he too was part of the jetsam of a title that "suited me as well as feathers on my bottom," as Colette put it—we did not speak much. After all, we were each a member of a species more or less unknown to the other. As I was going, Colette gave me her latest book, *Aventures quotidiennes,* with *For M.G., a distinguished adventurer* written in it. I did not consider myself either the one or the other, and I almost asked her for a dedication that fitted me better. But the worst of the matter was that I left the book lying on an armchair. Was this some piece of knavery (worthy of Scribe or Émile Augier) on the part of my subconscious so that I should not lose hold of Ariadne's thread? In her good-natured way, Colette sent me the book, together with this note: *For having forgotten this book (the '48 brandy, ha, ha!) you really deserve to have one of your dignities lopped off. Which do you prefer, "adventurer" or "distinguished"?*

A present of roses, which I sent with my apologies, allowed me to keep the relationship alive.

On the first floor, Colette had arranged a room after her own heart, and there she spent most of her time.

Both the walls and the ceiling were covered with a thick and rather dark glazed paper smothered with flowers. This same paper went with her in all her removals. But at the Palais-Royal it so darkened her first bedroom that she had it covered with a pale gray lining paper under which it could still be made out.

For callers there was a deep divan, quantities of cushions, soft rugs, and squat armchairs: generally Colette sat on the floor with her legs folded under her. Scattered all over the room there were millefiori paperweights and little things made of glass. No portraits, except for those of animals: she would never allow human forms in the place where she worked.

Evening after evening, we talked tirelessly on and on until late into the night. Sometimes I asked her direct blunt personal questions, and she never turned them aside. Except for literature, we talked about everything. I admired the way she applied the simplest solution, the most telling phrase, to every situation, every question. She gave me back a world of taste, smell, and natural shapes, a world that I had let drift away from me. And all this had great gaiety running through it—brilliant flashes of wit.

It was hard for me, but I opened my heart to her—a heart too long closed upon itself. I did not dare ask her how she felt about me, and she said nothing. Yet one night when I had come without my car she went with me as far as the cab that I had sent for. When I was already sitting in it, I murmured a few loving words, to which she made no reply. But she turned toward the driver, and with that roughness and familiarity that she often put on, she said, pointing at me, "Go on: cart it away . . . and take great care not to do it any harm."

For me those nights at Auteuil are still unequaled. But the past continually shows more and more of itself. It is only during these last years that I have come to know about Colette's letters to Marguerite Moreno, her closest friend, and that I have been able to make out the other leaf of the diptych. In comparison with a woman of this kind, endowed with every gift of language and every charm of mind, it seemed to me that I was a lumpish creature and I wondered what interest I could possibly have for her. And now I read, "I am waiting for my nightly storyteller." So I was Scheherazade, and I never knew it! And this, which surprised me even more: "Last night Goudeket and I had one of those conversations that begin at midnight and end at twenty-five past four in the morning. Yes. Would you believe it? How I love fencing with a certain degree of delicacy and finding that my partner understands with his antennae."

Antennae? Me, with my blundering great feet? This inordinate praise coming from one who more than anyone else on earth shared the subtle awareness of animals and touched, felt things as they do, and understood their way of speech. How strange and distressing it is to come to a forever ended dialogue and take it up again, to change it, almost. Forever: is there any certainty about that?

"What a masculine grace there is in a certain kind of softening, and how touching it is to see the inner fire melt the outer envelope. Don't you think there are very few men who know, without raising their voices or changing their tone, how to say . . . just the right thing?"

Yes, that envelope that I had hardened against myself was melting. In the bosom of a man approaching middle age, an adolescent's heart was stirring. But for too long I had checked the flood of loving words that rose to my lips, and I scarcely dared let them come out. And now I was being praised for my reticence!

On her side, she was not without anxieties. Was I not sixteen years younger than she? The letters to Marguerite Moreno show that she calculated the risks she ran and faced them with courage.

"What a shrewd lack of foresight there is in my actions!" she wrote that same month. And farther on:

"So you see you must not worry about me. From time to time I grow uneasy, I jump, I prick up my ears: 'Come now,' I call out to myself, and then deliberately stop thinking." And lastly: "No, I am not mad—it is far more serious than that."

If only I had known! How I would have thrown myself at her feet to reassure her! It would have been a wholly useless gesture, I may add: faithfulness is not something that can be declared; it can only be demonstrated—and its proof requires a great deal of time.

Naturally there was a general stir of curiosity about me. People wanted to know the man Colette looked upon with favor and to be the first to be able to talk about him. So, one blazing afternoon in June when I was with Colette in the little overcrowded garden at Auteuil, Madame de Noailles was announced, and we went to meet her. Her name had a glamour that is unimaginable today. Although Anna de Brancovan was born in Paris and had lived there, her origins provided her with a fascinating mystery, for she came to us from the shores of the Black Sea on her father's side, and from the Ionian on her mother's. Her marriage with a Noailles had necessarily brought her into society, and her first collection of verse had necessarily and immediately brought her to the attention of the public. *Le Coeur innombrable*—the title alone would have been enough to make the book reach even as far as the *chansonniers,* the people who sing in cafés. A vivid lyrical energy informs these poems, which have many happy lines; and some of them still sing in their readers' memories. I do not think they are destined to oblivion; and a little more severity would perhaps have preserved them from it. Anna de Noailles had a radiant personality and an utterly unique flow of words that turned her conversation into a monologue crammed with parentheses, conceits, and wild flights that held the field wherever she happened to be.

I had never met her. This unexpected encounter, happening at Colette's house, could not fail to make me feel extremely nervous. All at once she was there, slight, holding her head high, and dressed in something white and frothy that showed her charming little feet: there was her invariable fringe on her forehead, and her mouth had an ironic expression. She gave me her haughtiest glance, and obviously determined to make me vanish from the face of the earth by way of showing her power, she uttered these disconcerting words: "Monsieur, I am the most intelligent person of this century."

At that time I was unaware that this outrageous statement was meant less to astonish than to cover her shyness. What one assumes to be vanity on the part of those whose position depends upon an audience is generally no more than a desperate desire for reassurance. I wonder whether even Sacha Guitry, whose self-centeredness was real enough, was taking himself seriously when he paced up and down his library with a most laudatory article by Colette clutched in his fist and indignation breathing from his nostrils as he repeated, "And not a single use of the word genius, not a single one!"

There was indeed only one thing for me to do—crumble into dust. But my emotion produced the opposite effect: I heard myself insolently replying, in a calm voice that did not seem to belong to me, "I am all the happier to know it, madame, since up to this moment I had supposed that I occupied that position."

Madame de Noailles's eye, which up to that point had merely looked through me, focused upon my person. Henceforward I had an existence, a mass, a weight. As a champion fencer who happens to be touched by a beginner may cry "Touché" a little too loud, so she suddenly paid me a disproportionate amount of attention, and not five minutes later she was saying to me in the same breath, "My dear Maurice, and I forbid you to call me Anna . . ."

The contrast between the two writers was exceedingly striking: the one as slight as could be, soaring, aerial, calling clouds to mind and even perhaps on occasion lightning; the other compact, her feet well down on earth, deriving her strength and worth from nature. Their friendship, which was to blossom into a true and reciprocal affection, was then only at its beginning, and Colette watched Anna de Noailles with the minute attention that she would have devoted to a bright-feathered bird whose habits and behavior were unknown to her.

The calling up of one's memories has one strangely disturbing aspect: since you know what happened afterwards, the image of any given event is not entirely free from reflections thrown back upon it. Every day I feel more strongly that the future is not a chasm beyond which there exists nothing: the future is perhaps only one of various possible concepts of time. However that may be, ten years later Colette pronounced Madame de Noailles's eulogy before the Royal Belgian Academy and she quoted one of her remarks—a remark that I will now tell you about, so that you and I will step back to a time at which this speech of Colette's (now thirty years behind us) was still no more than a remote point in the future. I can see Colette again, and the royal blue and pink negligee that she was wearing; she left me standing there alone with Madame de Noailles and then came back from the garden and put a scented herb into her guest's hand, crumpling it so that "she should always have a sweet-smelling memory of the house."

"God above!" cried Anna de Noailles with her usual extravagance, "how good it smells. What is this unknown, splendid wonder?"

"It is just common balm," said Colette.

"Balm? So here it is at last, this balm that I have written so much about!"

As you see, she was by no means averse to humor, even when the laughter was at her expense; and later we had more than one instance of this. When she had gone, I said that I was very much surprised that a writer could make an effectual use of words that were no more than vague notions for her.

"That's her privilege as a poet," said Colette, "and I envy her for it. Everything that I have to find out, she can discover by intuition."

And now I chance upon a letter from Anna de Noailles to Colette, dated August 4, 1925, two months later, which recalls this scene—a scene whose meaning had not in fact escaped her.

For me your letter is filled with sage from the garden (or mint, or balm—you bewildered my Theocritean insight) because I never separate the idea of you from those enchanting bunches of leaves that you brought me and that make me love the deceptive earth—that earth which is so lovely on the surface and so horrible when it has robbed you of exquisite friends as it has robbed me. Send me postcards (how absurd) of your journey; or let the dear, subtle Maurice, precise and delicate acrobat with the exactly balanced word, post them to me during your days of splendid, tiring work.

The holidays were coming near. For August, Colette had agreed to make a theatrical tour, playing the character of Léa in the play that she and Léopold Marchand had adapted from her novel *Chéri*. For my part, I had rented a little villa at Guerrevieille for July; this was a little hamlet, a few houses on the side of a hill among the pines of Beauvallon on the bay of Saint-Tropez, and it was quite easy to persuade her to go there with me. She knew nothing of the South of France except for the Riviera of former days, that is to say, an artificial South with a pale winter sun, a country which gave itself spurious Italian airs, and in which there were to be seen courtesans in boas and grand-dukes, all bowling along in victorias, casinos, the Promenade des Anglais, Vogade's crystallized fruit, and the lingering shadow of the Prince of Wales and Marie Bashkirtsev.

Colette's meeting with Provence in the height of

the summer was like an instant and complete con-
quest. Myself, I had been quite won over by the country the year before: I had been staying in Brittany,
and after five days of rain that did not stop for a single
hour I grasped the steering wheel of my car and swore
I should never stop until I reached the sun. My oath
led me as far as Beauvallon: it was high time—a little
farther and I should have had to take to the sea. But
for Colette it was quite different: she was rediscovering a country that she had lost. It is well known that
her father and her paternal grandparents were born at
Toulon. The "captain," with his accent, his rotund
flow of speech, his wild notions, and his sobriety, had
always been a true Provençal. Colette had certainly
been able to adopt Le Crotoy, the Franche-Comté,
Brittany, and the Corrèze, each in turn; but this, almost as much as La Puisaye, was her real home.

She recognized all the scent-bearing trees and
bushes at once, investigating them more with her nose
than with her eyes, as a hound might do. We came
into the middle of a heat wave, which delighted her at
the same time that it made her gasp. The house was
minute. To heat our water, there was no fuel but pine
cones. At night we dragged our mattresses into the
open. Crickets, toads, tree frogs, little night birds:
nothing so full of sound as the nights of that summer.

Not a breath of air until the first dawn brought us its great puffs of sharp, resin-scented wind.

I was in a hurry to show Colette Saint-Tropez, and we went there the first day. It had not yet lost its virginity to tourism and it was still an easygoing little port, with nothing to foretell its extraordinary future. Colette was overcome directly. She at once decided to sell the place she still had at Rozven in Brittany and to buy another in the neighborhood of Saint-Tropez. I have never known anyone who made up her mind so quickly.

"At least give yourself time to think it over," I used to say to her sometimes.

"I *have* thought it over," she would reply.

Before the end of our stay, she had bought a little house called Tamaris-les-Pins; she had renamed it La Treille muscate and had made well-judged plans with contractors and craftsmen for its improvement. The land amounted to nearly five acres. Later I added an acre of vineyard that happened to come up for sale. But when we sold the little estate in 1938, its area was no more than three acres. A singular example of the steady shrinking of the earth's crust!

Saint-Tropez marks the place of the flowering of our relationship, our rapture, our greatest happiness in living. The hours flowed by, deep blue at night, all gold by day . . .

Sometimes we went to the Treille muscate for Christmas, less often in spring. Colette stayed there close on three months every summer, whereas I was obliged to leave Paris later than she and to go back earlier. I owe a great many letters to this difference in timing, and they bring back those splendid days even more clearly to my memory. This correspondence,

with its passionate, intimate, and occasionally un-
guarded aspects, cannot be published until many
years have passed. But since my task is to make an exceptional woman whose every facet is of importance
to the public better and better understood, I think it
my duty not to hold back for myself those extracts
that I can produce. I will only show you Colette in
her garden at Saint-Tropez with her pets—a kind,
simple, lively Colette.

So, until the time the pearl trade literally fell to
pieces under the weight of the American depression,
helped by the development of the Japanese cultured
pearl, Colette left for the South in my car, with the
chauffeur, a good month before me. I took the Blue
Train and got out at Saint-Raphaël. The first year Colette was not at the station, but the chauffeur handed
me a letter:

I have not come to meet you because I am too busy
trying to make the house look at least something like
a real house to welcome you. So, like the house, look
as if you were pleased when you see it, just to encourage me. You would never believe what it was like yesterday evening when they brought three loads of sand
to soften the harshness of the courtyard and I badgered
the painters to make them take away their buckets of
paint, brooms, wheelbarrows, and the biggest heaps of

rubble. And these windows still without curtains! I expect some pretty material for them next week. I am counting on you to help me, to help us, to water the young peach trees at half past nine in the evening. I am counting on you to look with a kindly eye upon all the little things I have done, those I like the best. I am counting on you—full stop.

She never dated her letters—less for me than for anyone else, so that putting them into date order will be very difficult. On the other hand, she did always put down the day and the time very exactly: "Tuesday, a quarter past four in the afternoon." "Oh, if only she had kept my letters to her," I often used to think after her death, "how much easier it would be to date hers, by cross-checking." Now, she had kept them all; but when I discovered them, to my astonishment I realized that I had behaved in exactly the same way: "Thursday, ten minutes past four." Fundamentally, that was the only thing that mattered to us, to place the other in the exact time in which the letter was being written.

Because of the tone of voice and the minute details that have meaning for me alone, it is probable that only I can arrange these letters in chronological order; but they still have such an evocative power over me that I cannot bring myself to look upon them as a subject for analysis. Again, I could have and I ought to have left them in their postmarked envelopes. One ought always to keep the envelopes of a correspondence, if only from the point of view of a more practical aspect—that of the writing. But in my relationship with Colette I never at any time looked upon her as a famous person whose slightest scrap of writing should be preserved. How many notes, rough drafts, pages of manuscript have vanished in the wastepaper basket! If I had behaved otherwise, our relationship would not have had that fine careless freedom that must exist for a man and woman to be happy together. In the same way, there are many pieces of information about Colette's past history that are lacking: her biographers will have to search for them with great pains, whereas I could just have asked her. Yet this would have meant bringing something deliberate, calculated, into our ordinary, everyday life together, as well as the idea that it might some day come to an end!

But there is no doubt about the date of the following letter. It comes just after the first time I left Saint-Tropez, in September of 1926.

You will scarcely believe it, but it is only nine o'clock and I am writing to you already. It is the first time you have left me behind in this house, and your absence has left such an emptiness that I thought of settling down on the terrace rather than coming here.

I have done a little watering; I dined on a piece of bread rubbed with garlic, and a peach, like a peasant of the old days; and I have been listening to our people.

Louise [the caretaker of the little estate]: Oh, this weather! Dear God, this weather! You can't have three fine days together before it turns horrible!

Myself: How do you mean, horrible?

Louise: Why, this dreadful wind, of course!

The animals are unbearable. Souci [the bulldog bitch] above all. She is cherishing her grief, and it grows nonetheless. There is nothing to be done to make her laugh. She does nothing but weep. A face all blubbered. When they went out first thing this morning, they both [the she-cat and Souci] went into the "little forest" and sat there facing the house door that never opened. Do they suppose it's any fun for me either? They are dreadful creatures, animals. They have no reticence, no decency, in their sorrow. . . .

This morning it is Saint Anne's fair; three days of fair. We went at nine o'clock and I could not resist some of those baubles that tempt frivolous creatures like me—hedge-trimming shears, a hone, and some scissors for cleaning up the flower beds. These weaknesses of mine will be nothing new to you! . . .

. . . I am taking back the little desk, the place I gave you. I almost took back your yellow paper. What don't I take away from you? It seems to me that already I have taken a great deal. I have deprived you of part of the "future views" that you might have had.

But perhaps it was just as well that you did not keep them, and that I have removed them like a thorn. . . .

. . . My dear, the weather is lovely—and it is fine as a matter of course, so much as a matter of course. What shall I tell you about? Nothing about me: I just go from bathing to eating, from eating to the shore, from the shore to bed, and from bed to my blue paper. The white tomcat, deceived by the color, hurled herself upon our Chatte, our trusting, marvelous Chatte! Scratched, routed, trembling, she could not understand, for tomcats *do not set upon she-cats,* and the attack had been unspeakably fierce. I sent the white tom flying with a timely kick, but yesterday poor pretty Chatte did not want to come with me any more. This morning I took her for a protected walk, with a guard of honor, policemen on bicycles, plainclothes men, the lot, and she is growing easier in her mind. . . .

I have found a splendid angora caterpillar adorned with such long hairs that the wind plays through them as it does over a field of corn! I took the caterpillar away from Kro [the magnificent tom of the same breed as Chatte], who was patting the creature's wool with his paws—a wool even more angora-ish than his. I took it clean away—and the word clean . . . I have to comb this village beau (he will only dip his fingers in the washbasin) and take seventy-five fleas off him, as well as a thousand droppings of the same, spikes of grass, snails, bits of broken bottle, rocks, and coconuts —you know that my love of exact research never allows the least exaggeration.

For your new study, would you like a capital brand-new Louis XV piece from Antony Mars [an antique dealer in Saint-Tropez]? He has just brought back a Louis XIV Moustiers cruet with a black background—shouldn't we make the most of this opportunity? It is a pure gem, and you would swear that at the utmost it was a fortnight old; whereas in fact it is all of six weeks. . . .

Chatte's chronicle. She is quite impossible either to paint or to describe. She is all love and loving looks. She is convinced that she is in kit, and to house her family she asks for everything that is to be had by way of lodgings for cats—the drawers in the chest, the shelves in the big cupboard, my bedroom, and the terrace. As I am writing to you now, she is pressed against my side and she never stops talking. It is early. . . .

At last Chatte has been brought to bed. I have not told you these last days that I was worried about her. Her belly was too small and soft. And yesterday morning I felt in vain for some movement in that too-soft belly. I said to Pauline, "She has one dead kitten and perhaps none alive." And I was afraid of infection. Yesterday afternoon she began to mew and cry. Nothing came. Only at ten in the evening yesterday did she push out one dead kitten in very bad shape and a pretty little striped one alive. The dead kitten had to be taken away very quickly, for she already looked upon it as part of the mess and she was beginning to eat it. The pretty little striped one came afterwards. It was close on midnight when Pauline finished cleaning up our Chatte, who is very well and has no fever. I hope the journey will not upset her too much. You will find little Stripes a handsome kitten, and we will give him a name. They gave me the basket of cats this morning, and Chatte drank a gallon of warm milk.

No one should be surprised at the amount of space these letters devote to Chatte, "the one who declined any other name, as though there were only one she-cat on earth." Just as in her novel *La Chatte* Colette supposed that a she-cat might divide husband and wife, destroying their relationship, so this one provided still another link between us. For although today (since I am not really a country person, nor yet a gardener) part of the fairyland that Colette led me into has vanished for me, I was born with the feeling I have for the nation of cats. I love their secrecy, and in their eyes of molten gold I think I can read a nostalgia for the remote forests they left not so very long ago. Sometimes, during the dreary, stagnant period of my too-prudent youth, I used to liken myself to them. Walking vaguely through the warm night in the streets of Paris, alone, a prey to my indecision, I have more than once met with a cat, a wanderer too, and I have entered into conversation with it. I have picked it up, gone with it to the nearest bar that was open and treated it to a saucer of milk, and then I have taken it back to the place where I found it. At the beginning I was stiff and formal, but Colette soon discovered this weakest point in my armor. We bought Chatte together at a show where neither one nor the other could resist her gaze. For thirteen years she gave us her soul, the small, wise, ardent soul of an animal, loving both of us equally. For Colette, then, it was not merely that she was telling me of Chatte's doings great and small; she was touching upon what was in a way the most secret, intimate side of our relationship—one of the strongest bonds in a union that was to bear no fruit.

It is nine o'clock. Nothing new. Everything is new. . . .

A splendid night: yes, indeed! Before sunrise a storm, a heavy storm, that stopped only to begin once more. Am I never going to be able to sleep again? And at eight o'clock, with God's own thunder and blinding rain pouring down, Chatte was not to be found. Never were divers searching for sunken treasure as soaked as we. And my hair was growing white and the kitten was hungry. Explorations that discovered nothing. I was desperate, and after two and a half hours I did as I sometimes do: I took a firm hold of myself and forced myself to practice divination; and I said, "She is in the house." Everything was searched and searched again— the wall closet, cupboards, wardrobes, the lumber room, the refrigerator, under the stairs, the well. Then I went into what had been my bedroom, now appropriated by our daughter, and I listened with all my might during a lull in the rain and I heard a hardly recognizable tiny voice that called out just once, for Chatte has not yet recovered her voice. I leaped to the little drawer of the little chest and I extracted my poor flattened Chatte, out of her mind with anxiety, and half-smothered, and I carried her back to her basket. My dear, just think of that poor shut-in creature who could hear us calling her name and could not make herself heard! The way she thanked me in her basket —you really should have been there, to have had your heart wrung. She wouldn't allow me to leave her for a minute.

But when you come to think of it, what was the bloody fool doing in that drawer? I think the half-witted, scoundrelly blockhead of a cat must have been frightened by the thunder, as she was last year, and she hid in the darkest place she could find.

. . . Would you like some well-turned phrases? Listen to the beginning of this tale, told by Louise [the caretaker]. "I meet Étienne [a gardener], and he says to me, 'You wouldn't like to be a godmother, I suppose?' 'Where's the christening?' says I. 'At my place,' says he. 'Well,' says I, 'I never knew you were a father before being married.' 'It's not a baby,' he says, 'it's my calf.' A calf! So then I says to him, 'Well, thank you very much,' I says, etc., etc." What do you think of our elegance? . . .

I am writing to you from Chatte's courtyard, which I live in more and more as the sun changes its course. It is perhaps a little less hot, and the western air is fresher. And what about Paris? And you? But this cannot go on. I am resting after a furiously active morning. I was out of doors at six; and six o'clock is a very fine time of day. Climbed up one side of Borély and dropped down on the other; wandered about; stole some incomparable figs. Then, harvesting grapes at the Vanders'. Sticky, covered with dust, filthy, I had a shower and now I am clean: I am no longer toiling with the sun right overhead. It is eleven. Opposite me, asleep, there is a little bulldog creature that never stops loving you and being sorry that you are not here. This morning, as she made her ritual objections to taking a walk and refused to leave the doorstep where she was waiting for you, I took her in my arms and comforted her; but I was mean enough to murmur into her ear, "You are waiting for Maurice." She flung herself with all her strength in the direction of the house with such a cry that I too felt the wound. Until now you did not know that a bitch was worth loving and taking care of.

Hearing your voice fills me with evil feelings. In reach and out of reach at the same time. Oh, how I hate that telephone! Don't forget to ring me up on Wednesday. I am being unreasonable; but it is hard, living in such a delightful place without you. . . . The sea was still warm this morning, but a bout of mistral is stirring it up and the sky is clouding over. Yesterday evening we were told that there was to be a change in the weather by clouds of butterflies, — so many butterflies that nobody thought it funny any more. They crowded the glasses and the plates and hid the lamps and the air was filled with the hail-like *noise* of their wings. Even the cats no longer thought it funny.

I lived in a ground-floor flat at the corner of the rue de Lubeck; it was shaped like a slice of cheese, and the considerable slope of the avenue du Président-Wilson raised some of it above ground level. It was lit by eight windows, or rather by seven, for one was false and it was only there so that the beholder's sense of symmetry should not be jarred. As well as the front door in the avenue du Président-Wilson and the servants' entrance, it had a private door on to the rue de Lubeck, which gave me the look of someone I really did not resemble in the least—a kind of Casanova who might send one mistress stealing away from this door while another came in through the other. It was somewhat too big a flat for a bachelor; it was carefully furnished, and in spite of myself I had turned it into my own reflection—rather too solemn and devoid of any bold stroke of taste. Like me, it deserved to be shaken up a little: Colette promised to see to it for me, but the place intimidated her.

Before seeing Colette again, I had taken it into my head to fill a gap in my education: I can scarcely do without music, but I cannot play at all. (I have a sister, four years younger than myself. I have not happened to speak of her until now. Her name is Stella;

she lives for music and nothing else, and she has become well known.) So I hired a grand piano, had it put in my anteroom, so as not to upset the exact arrangement of the rest of the furniture, and summoned a *demoiselle de piano,* as they say in Belgium. Of course I had to begin with scales. Scales up and scales down: Lord, what quantities of scales I played, at thirty years of age and more! Alas, you need the nimble fingers of a child. As for reading, I did manage to get right through a few pieces for six-year-old virtuosos; but under my doubtful hands they all assumed the air of a funeral march.

My neighbor upstairs was the great actress Gabrielle Dorziat, whom I occasionally saw as she left the house. Since then I have often met her. Yet it was not until a little while ago that I ever had a long enough talk with her for her to be able to ask me, "But who was the child who practiced the piano in your flat?"

"It was I, my dear," I replied, looking down.

This was the flat from which I telephoned Colette.

So you have gone . . . I try to make out where you are now; it is half past nine; the sky is brightening a little, and so am I. The animals are coming back from the vineyard and the beach, with Pauline. I am writing to you so that you shall find something other than a wooden-faced telegram when you arrive. I must possess my soul in patience, and possess it without you

. . . This country ceases to be entirely comprehensible when you are not here with me. . . .

. . . Page 204. You left me at page 196 [Colette was working on *La Naissance du Jour*], at the very moment I myself abandoned that same page 196 to fly to the rescue of 177 et seq., which were calling out aloud for me. That respresents a great many hours, a great deal of doubt, and a great deal of the stiffness that comes from sitting. Such a long scene between two characters ought (1) not to hide the fact that it is long, and (2) not to seem too long. . . .

Yesterday evening, just after sunset, in the pure, mistral-swept sky, there appeared an immense cloud, a vast object that made one feel like a primitive soul with a strong desire to run away and hide. Never before have I gazed from so near upon such a monster; it was brown, with huge folds, and it was more solid than a mountain, unsmudged except for a little grayish fur where it turned in; it had a belly, two bellies, three bellies, a tortoise's neck and a mouth that very slowly opened. It lay just above the mistral, motionless or almost so, during a storm that blew for several hours. And there was nothing else but this monster in the sky. If there had been a savage here, or Conan Doyle, what howlings we should have heard!

It was in 1927 that Colette wrote *La Naissance du Jour*. How good she was to work so, when everything was calling her out of doors! She wrote in the afternoon, after a short siesta, in the main room of the house; it was on the ground floor and it looked out over the sea, though from quite a long way off. The closed shutters preserved her both from the glare and from her own longing to escape. She rarely spoke confidentially about her writing, and it is only in her letters that one can surprise her at work. Page 196: the ending is at hand; she is soon going to be delivered from this persistent throbbing anxiety that haunts her days and breaks in upon her nights! Yes, but her characters have started to behave in a way that she could not foresee, and what they say on page 177 now rings false in her ears. Back, back, quickly she turns back: and how many times after that was she to go over and over the earlier pages?

. . . For, although I worked better here, I am not working so well now; I have been without you too long. And then, I have to know what you think of the piece with Vial in it: it is still pestering me, although it is finished. Between now and the time I leave, I shall still be guilty of a few pages. I almost achieved 209 yesterday. But I am not counting my long casting-back, the tightening up, the changing, etc.

It is generally supposed that the character of Vial portrays me, and I must admit that it is an easy mistake to make. Because it simplified matters when she was writing *La Naissance du Jour,* Colette depicted herself in the very place she was describing. All her characters, including Vial, were based upon the people around her there. And yet the book is fiction, for the feelings that Colette expresses in it were not her own. She was indeed compelled to imagine the attitudes and the utterances of a woman who renounced love well on in her life, for they were entirely the contrary of her own.

To be sure, the words "I am not working so well now; I have been without you too long" could mean "I need to have my model at hand"; but she is really speaking of that interchange that every writer wants with someone near to him, even if it is only his maid, as it was for Molière. And Colette would never have said that she was eager to know what I thought of the piece about Vial if I had been in any way concerned.

One summer more, still one more summer. I find them more and more precious, more heart-touching than ever, these summers with you. A more sensible woman than I would take her head in both hands and cry out aloud. Thank God, thank the devil, I am not a more sensible woman than myself.

How pathetic these lines seem to me, now that I reread them today. Since the problem of the difference of age in a pair has virtually no existence for the man, the passage did not strike me when I first read it.

Can it be that this question obsessed Colette up until the placid days of the end of her life, without my really ever being aware of it because of my male short-sightedness? "Next spring," she says in another letter to me, "will you still be my friend? It is so many years since I bothered at all about my next spring."

It is true that the danger of a middle-aged woman's losing the young companion she loves—a risk that some of her characters refuse to accept—is a theme that runs through the whole of Colette's work. She was only thirty-six when she wrote *La Vagabonde*. Ten years later, in *Chéri,* her masterpiece, she developed this theme to its fullest extent: Léa proudly accepts the danger and indeed overcomes it up until the time of the break that Colette regarded as inevitable. In *La Naissance du Jour,* of course, it is paradoxically eluded. As for the heroine of *Le Képi,* she is so stupid that she is hardly aware of the danger.

The search for personal references in Colette's work may seem uncommonly easy; but I do urge upon her future commentators a care that is in direct proportion to this apparent ease. Scarcely will they have discovered a model for the character of Chéri somewhere about 1920 than they will find that the first drafts of *Chéri* date from 1911. It is true that a young man who was close to Colette at that time did provide most of Chéri's characteristics, but she did not have the slightest intention of referring to herself when she wrote the tales called *Clouk* and *Chéri*. At that period she moved about among demimondaines a great deal —a world in which couples like Léa and Chéri were commonplace—and she had only to look around her: the blond, plump, respectably dissolute creature, a good sort and at the same time a really strong character, who caught her eye and served as the basis for Léa, was called Suzanne Derval.

For my part, I think that although a writer's personal obsessions shape his work, the work often has its own effect back on the writer. More than one author has ended up by imitating his characters, or else his fate has seen to it that he does. My nature and the circumstances of my childhood required that I should fall passionately in love with a woman who possessed the glamour of fame, so that I could lay the garland of my too-long-repressed ardor at her feet; and it was very probable that such a woman would be older than I. Indeed, who can tell whether I, having been (no doubt by my own fault) disappointed of the maternal wing that I longed for, was not still dimly searching for it?

As for Colette, it is true that much later she wrote the words, "When I was building up the character of Léa, a forewarning"—and indeed I have known her to have astonishing premonitions, instinctive foresights so exact that some passages in her books seem to be an account of what had already happened to her, whereas in fact the writing preceded the event. Still I cannot be sure whether it was chance that for a good third of her life she at least seemed to be in the position of her main heroine or whether she owed it to the influence that creations have upon their creators.

For a long while she believed that our relationship would necessarily come to the same end as those in her books—would obey the same laws. What a pity that I never suspected this! For I looked upon myself as extraordinarily fortunate that such a woman should trouble with me at all, and on my side I thought that I could only figure briefly in her life. So both of us, for ten years on end, avoided mentioning a closer relationship which would have made us both very happy. It was only at Saint-Tropez that we really lived together, and that is why Saint-Tropez was so important to us. After the boulevard Suchet, Colette moved first to the rue de Beaujolais, but on the mezzanine that time, while I still went on living in the avenue du Président-Wilson. Gradually we came closer together. I had to give up my flat because of the ruin of my business, and I took a room at Claridge's, next to Colette's. Two years later we rented adjoining sets of chambers in the rue de Marignan. Changing my trade, I took to journalism, a refuge that gave me all that I could ask for. And there we were, both Colette and I, commissioned (though on different planes) to give an account of the *Normandie*'s first crossing of the Atlantic. How were we going to manage to stay together in the prudish United States?

"If we were to marry," I said, laughing, "there would be no problem." Colette looked up at me and suddenly I realized all that this binding, this consolidation of our relationship meant to her. So it was as a married couple that we waved to the Statue of Liberty and as honeymooners that we toured New York.

. . . Yesterday Chatte suddenly turned into a puma and bounded upon something alive that struggled furiously, just there on the edge of the terrace, before my eyes. It was a large, magnificent green lizard, dressed in emeralds, opals, and enamel—a marvel! I leaped in my turn to take him away from her: he was terribly angry and he opened his splendid little crimson jaws. But I had been a lizard before ever he was, and I managed to get him from my wicked, lovely Chatte. He was only a little bitten at the root of his tail; I took advantage of his rage to give him some drops of water to drink—he drank them beautifully. I stroked him, scratched his head, and patted his back in the midst of Louise's bawling and horrified swooning. And then I carried him a long way off in the vineyard, where he vanished in a flash of green light. He, or rather she, went to tell her family all about it; and no doubt the family shrugged its shoulders . . .

Yesterday evening I produced the last of the season's ravioli. And to cap my sadness and my longing for you, so dreadful a wind got up that we had to carry our plates into the little room that we call the dining room. And then we went to have a look at Palmyre's, the only place that has kept the charm of our Saint-Tropez of former days. There is the player piano. And the old man who collects the pennies. And a few men who could dance well, and who scorned the women: you really should have seen their faces.

What else shall I tell you . . . ? I forgot to say that in this dancing pit of Palmyre's there was a little village girl, about seven or eight, in a pink dress, and all through all the dances she weaved and glided everywhere between the couples, possessed by the spirit of the dance; and all by herself she made perfectly charming steps, paying no attention to anyone, with one little hand in the air as though she were leaning on a ghostly shoulder. A ravishing and a disturbing sight. In the end a local man danced with her—"Just once round, eh?"—and nothing at all was left of her spontaneous grace.

Dinner at Géraldy's with the Jacques Chardonnes— he wrote *L'Épithalame*. That villa makes me throw up as I stand. It is the work of two simple creatures, Lebout [an architect and Géraldy's brother-in-law] and Géraldy. But it is really very sweet. Not a bad evening —we needed overcoats on the terrace.

. . . I am a water-diviner. And a water-diviner to the utmost pitch of sorcery! I am transported with pride, fatuous pride! Today Mme Aude took Véra and me to see her unfinished house, up there on the

slope beyond the Schroeders. A site and an unfinished
house, both of them splendid, a wonderful opportunity
for anyone who wanted to finish the house and bring
off a good business deal. Sextia Aude told me that she
had discovered two or three wells on the property,
thanks to her gifts as a dowser! "But how is it done?"
She cut the first fork of mimosa that came to hand
and showed me how it turned in her grasp. "Have a
go," she said. "If you have the gift, you will feel it at
once." Ah! . . . what an extraordinary sensation! As
I came near to the water the fork came alive between
my hands, more alive, self-willed, and it twisted like
a snake. Véra tried: she is less of a dowser than I, but
she has something of it. As you can very well imagine,
as soon as I was back here I roused up Louise and
Pauline; but the fork would not move in their hands.
So at last I have a livelihood. When the dowsing curé
of the Haute-Vienne was sent for to find a spring, he
asked twenty-five thousand francs when there was
water, and five hundred francs for his expenses when
there was none. . . .

I am much put about by this revelation. How about
you? You had better remain modest, just modest.
Lovely spring, how could you expect my fork not to
turn?

My dear, last year one thousand six hundred liters
of wine were made altogether. This year, with the
vineyard reduced by a third, we have made more than
one thousand two hundred! And such wine! I tasted
the must this morning: it is pure sugar, that is, poten-
tial alcohol. Between a thousand and a thousand one
hundred liters of red, ninety liters of white in three

carboys, and one carboy of rosé to see what it will be like. And yesterday we cooked a little demijohn of ratafia [wine and brandy], and yesterday evening at half past ten, in the garden, the cooked wine was still bubbling in its witch's caldron in the open air! Oh, how insane it is that you should have left so early! What a lovely vintage you would have had! The grapes are so good that one thousand six hundred kilos of them have given more than twelve hundred liters of wine.

"A woman," wrote Colette once, "belongs to as many countries as she has had happy love affairs." That is not quite true for a man, who, even in a relationship so exceptional as ours in its difference of age and value, is still the one who takes the initiative. It could seem to me that I had given Colette Provence as a dowry, as Charles V might have done if he happened to possess it. The sight of her blossoming out so magnificently there filled me with such immense happiness that in spite of my unfitness for country tasks I took pleasure in trying to do them at Saint-Tropez. I helped in the grape harvest when it took place, as it sometimes did, at the beginning of September. I agreed that the tainted stench of compost was pleasant, I memorized the names of bushes and flowers, and I learned how to examine them most searchingly. I could tell the birds by the way they flew. Unlike Colette, I did not reach the point of conversing with epeirids and other kinds of spiders, but I did become interested in the lives of insects. I agreed to preserve some that seemed to me exceptionally unpleasant and to destroy others that I thought handsome and even likable, such as the rose chafers in their bronze armor. Alas, when the magician goes, the spells are no longer there. A townsman I was, and a townsman I have become once more. As for the sciences, so for country matters: there is a kind of innate ignorance. Still I do derive some comfort from the fact that I have known worse than myself. Pierre Lazareff knows that I love him dearly, and I hope that he will forgive me for bringing up his name at this point. When I was a journalist and on the staff of *Paris-Soir,* I was going through his office one day (all the rooms in the building communicated with one another) to get to the editorial side. Although he was already very highly placed at that time, Pierre Lazareff still often wrote articles, and he was in the act of dictating a piece on the army maneuvers that were then going on. "Hidden among the waving heads of the ripe corn," came to my ears, whether I liked it or not. I stopped abruptly, with my hand on the doorknob. "But do you realize that it is March, Pierre?" I said.

"Yes. Why?"

"I don't think corn is ripe in March."

Pierre Lazareff chewed his inevitable pencil, shifted his spectacles, gazed right into my eyes, and with his characteristic thirst for exact information, asked me, "Are you quite sure?"

This morning I helped at Julio's [Julio van der Henst, our nearest neighbor, on the other side of the Salins road]. There is so much to do and to pick and there is no one to be hired, so they are conscribing the Desachys and the Couvenberghs: there is no labor to be had, for the entire countryside is in the vineyards— a glorious sight. The carboys of white wine, our carboys, are spewing that thick filth that so horrified you last year. As true as the fact that I love you, it is only being together that can console me for leaving this country—our country. Even if it means your ruin, my dear, you must spend September here.

Two hundred and ten pages of proof [*Le Voyage égoïste*] to correct today. How am I supposed to get on with my novel?

. . . I still go on dowsing, with the help of any forked twig I come across. I don't know how "they" explain this turning of the rod, but every time it lives and struggles in my hands I am thunderstruck. My coming near underground water wakes it up, and it goes to sleep again as I move away from the invisible spring. How beautiful it is, something that you do not understand!

Afterwards I often saw Colette, barefoot, wielding her divining rod. You would have said that it was some priestess carrying out a sacred rite. Since her childhood, springs had filled her with wonder and even with a desire to possess them. They continually recur in her works, and her two last books are studded with them. It is not surprising that feeling them tremble beneath her, bringing them to life, as it were, should send her into a trance.

But she did not want to know any more about it. It is impossible to deny the existence of sorcery (was it Colette who invented the word?). Sextia Aude, who revealed Colette's gift to her, could tell the exact place, depth, and even the quantity of the water by the number of times the rod turned, and some other indications, and she offered to tell Colette about it; but Colette would have none of it, for fear the mystery should seem less mysterious.

She possessed both a lively appetite for the supernatural and a basic inability to let it remain supernatural. So often she fought with all her might against the irresistible need to investigate which she knew was part of her nature. "How beautiful it is, something that you do not understand!" Sometimes it is only a paperweight, an optical illusion. Above all, do not oblige me to understand it!

It was for this reason too that she liked any kind of foretelling of the future; and she did not always refrain from experiments that came close to spiritualism. "Do you believe in it, then?" I asked her one day. The answer that she gave me may perhaps provide the key to many questions that have been asked about her: "Whether I believe in it or I don't believe in it doesn't make the slightest difference as far as I am concerned."

. . . After that, we went to see the Sedep villa for a certain Sacha Sforza, who might possibly take it. . . . And—my heart is still swollen with tears inside me— a cat . . . a cat that has been waiting for three weeks on the threshold. There is no caretaker. The cat (very well fed, no doubt by the neighbors) threw herself upon us, mistaking who we were, with *cries* of hope and of pain, and guided us from room to room with senseless words, questions, pitiful wailing. It was appalling. She went with us, crying out, as far as the door; then she fell silent, sat there without a word, and returned to her guard duty and her waiting. If I had not seen that she was in good physical shape, I should have carried her off by force. This is the kind of drama you can understand. So now I long for you even more, since that cat.

Yes, she had eventually succeeded in making me share her passionate curiosity about everything that belonged to the animal or vegetable kingdoms. At least that is what I thought. But not, as she said herself, her "complicity" with everything that moved and breathed. And even the word "complicity" is not strong enough. In her most fundamental being, Colette belonged to the earth, its essences and its secrets; and it was from there that she drew her strength, her *vertu,* as Louise would have said, for the Provençal caretaker spoke a French that was very near to its Latin origins. Colette not only knew the distinguishing marks and the habits of every creature, but when she was in contact with them she became a member of the same species, she had the same nature, shaped by the same forces. And if she foresaw their reactions and understood the most delicate shades of their language, it was because for the moment these reactions and this language were her own.

An intuitive understanding of her profound sympathy with every living creature is essential to anyone who wishes to make a true analysis of Colette's works. To my surprise and delight, I have found this foreknowledge in a study that has recently been sent to me—a study in the nature of a thesis. Its author is a young Swiss student, and it is entitled *Le sens panique chez Colette.* I would be very happy to go further with the theme that this young lady has begun so well; but my role must only be that of a witness, and not of an expounder.

During the first winter after it had been bought, we came to supervise the putting in order of La Treille muscate. We took up our lodgings in the little Hôtel

Sube, which looks over the port on the far side of the impressive statue of the Bailli de Suffren. One particularly silent night—and I do not think that nowadays these words can possibly be applied to Saint-Tropez in any season—Colette suddenly got up. "What's the matter?" I asked her. "Are you not feeling well?" She did not reply, and I looked at her in alarm. Listening intently, her face dark, she threw on her clothes. I repeated my question.

"Can't you hear?" she said at last, without moving her head. "He is drowning."

"A man?" I cried, leaping out of bed.

"No, no," she said, shrugging, "a dog, of course."

Now I too listened: I heard nothing more than a faint barking, a barking that came again; but I could not attach any exact meaning to it. Still less could I tell where it was coming from.

Colette had already gone. I felt so stupid that at first it never occurred to me to follow her, but I opened one side of the window and saw her running towards the place on the left-hand side of the harbor where the quay slopes down. By the time I had put on a dressing gown and hurried down the stairs, she was already coming back, rather breathless, with the front of her wrapper covered with dust and straw. I went to meet her. Fortunately it was a warm night.

"How long had he been swimming?" she said. "For

hours, maybe. He must have fallen into the water. Unless someone threw him in: can you ever be sure what people will do? Of course he couldn't manage to climb the sheer side of the quay. I only had to lie flat, and then leaning over a little I got him by the scruff. He was exhausted: a fox terrier crossed with God knows what! He had had all he could take."

She looked fiercely round the windows of the houses that ringed the harbor and added, "And not a soul would have stirred!"

"I must admit that I . . ."

"Yet what he was saying was perfectly clear."

Chatte-Chatte-Chatte still lies in the middle of your beret. So do I. I told Louise about the cat at the Sedep villa; she burst into tears and went to find out about her from a neighbor there. Petit-Kapeûk [one of Chatte's sons] drank a hogshead of milk this morning: we let him do it to see how far he would go. He did not "go" far. He made three stiff-legged paces to get clear of the last bowl, belched, and spewed it all out. And he gazed at the result as though he were saying, "What a pity!" He was made to be ashamed. I know that this tribal gossip will not bore you. . . .

I had a delightful note from Anna de Noailles, who, she says, certainly loves me. This morning, from eight until ten o'clock, I played the woodcutter and trimmed my forest. So my handwriting staggers a little. I did not set about it with a fainthearted billhook.

. . . There was a prodigious storm. In the garden the lightning struck a wire from the motor, and it went off with an astonishing bang that could be heard above the din overhead and the roaring of the wind. Flood, house under water, etc., etc. That is not very serious. But the whole district is without electricity—all the fuses blown, darkness and desolation. I managed to drive down and come back with a can of kerosene, although it is Sunday. And all that—but it amounts to nothing. What really prevented me from writing to you was that the moment everything began, I ran to call Chatte! Gusts of wind, huge drops, the deluge: no Chatte! I ran from the balcony to the terrace—there was already enough water swilling about to sweep me into the gulf—and I saw the unhappy Chatte on the ridge tiling of the courtyard tower. A blast of wind literally plucked her off and flung her down. I ran, I called Pauline and Louise, and we searched—no Chatte! Ten times during the long, incessant storm we went out to look for her, for I was afraid that as she is in kit she might have fallen awkwardly and hurt herself. We passed three and a half hours without news of her. It was only a quarter of an hour ago, in a lull, that she was able to get back, soaked through, and so pleased at reaching home again! As you can imagine, I dried her well, and she has eaten and she is here now, sitting on my paper. Are you happy? So am I.

The great drama of Chatte lost in the storm and threatened with death, and the women of the household running in every direction in the wind-blown rain, occurred at least once every season. I accept the risk of repetition rather than deprive the reader of Colette's always varying description.

Who has ever heard of a Perrasimi? [She is referring to Père Rasimi. The Rasimis were hereditary impresarios and organizers of café-concerts.] But I have: dear God, I have! More than once, he was my boss at the Éden in Lyons [when Colette acted in music halls, that is, between 1908 and 1912], and other places I forget. He was not at all like his son. A hard-faced slave driver. At Lyons, one evening, he forbade me to "hang about on the stage during the other numbers"; I said "Sh–" and he wanted to fine me *a hundred francs*. I told him, "I'll gouge out one of your eyes anyway, and we can discuss things later." A hundred francs! I was only earning a hundred and fifty!

. . . But yesterday was still another hellish orgy in the romantic manner [Chatte was in season]. Stripes, quite worn out, has had his place taken by the invincible Raton, who can make love on a wire, in a mulberry tree, on a balustrade, a roof, a wistaria, a pine, and really I forget how many other places. But this morning the wind is not in that quarter at all. She was on the balustrade and he was below, cooing—but already she was paying attention to nothing but the landscape. After breakfast she took her broad-brimmed hat trimmed with wild roses and her shepherdess's basket and she waited for me to go for a walk with her. What a hellion! And now she is a strictly upper-class cat.

. . . Lord, that you should have gone away before the nightingales! There are almost as many as at Marrakech! And I am sure you understand how I prize a clump of trees, for the sake of the birds. Yesterday, while I was getting wood, they were all there, just over my head. This summer I shall have a cement basin made for them: they will be short of fresh clean water. If only you could hear them: just by me, there is an explosion of nightingales, the long kiss of the titmice, and the chaffinches and the marsh warbler. All of them in their refuge, which is the little wood.

. . . This morning I found an unhappy great bombyx moth which had been struggling since the rain, for it had two of its wings and its feet stuck in the wet ground, and the rest of it free. I helped it out, instead of killing it, that breeder of caterpillars.

No letter yesterday! That hollows my day out like a funnel. What shall I tell you? That Mistraou has got up and that he is blowing. Not furiously, but he can change in no time at all. Lamponi [the caretaker who succeeded Louise] greeted his coming with tears of rage: "That shit-eater has come. I am going to bed, and I am going to cry all day!" The little tribes of these parts are very odd indeed.

Our Chatte! This morning, as I was coming back from looking at the black, foam-torn sea, at the gate I found a sad little puff of blue smoke that was being buffeted in every direction—Chatte, who had come to look for me right out there! She went off, reassured, with the mistral behind her, like a runaway lioness. . . .

A convolvulus with wild blue flowers has climbed up a tall pink geranium. If only you could see it! And since I have tidied up the petunias and the geraniums I am scent and nothing else.

. . . I ran over an old man this afternoon. The old man is Giraud's father: seventy-nine. He had got out, and in order to chat with a young imbecile some ten years his junior, he chose the middle of the road at the corner between the Place des Lices and the rue Allard. I saw two men talking in the roadway—you know Père Giraud's splendid presence—I hooted and expected some movement on their part. Nothing of the sort. I put the car out of gear, but I touched one of them, the oldest, who instantly fell to the ground, dragging the other down with him! I thought they were dead and I was terrified, above all when I recognized Père Giraud. He was carried home, and I to the police station, fortunately just at hand, where I met with some degree of kindness. . . . Later, I went to ask after my victim and I told his wife the story. Surprise, joy! She burst out, "Madame, what he deserves is a sound box on the ear! What, in the Place des Lices? And in the roadway? He has lied to me again; and he is always escaping!" (Etc., etc.)

. . . How could I have said no news Yesterday at about six there appeared Jouve, the engraver, in his car. He brought me a handsome Japanese vellum copy of *Les Paradis terrestres* [by Colette]. Altogether the general effect is fine, cold, and I admit it is an excellent edition. But that is nothing. In his car he had a leopard from Lake Chad, like a more beautiful version of the one I had, for this one will be bigger (she is six or seven months old) and she has miraculously short ears, and such fur. . . . There is nothing to come up to that golden coat marked with a thousand pure black spots. Her face, too, is finer, more noble and "wild beast" than the one I had. When I had shut up all the creatures here, I went to join her on the road; she was on a lead, with two maids who do nothing but look after her, and she was playing at attacking everything that went by. She hurled herself at my bare legs and we played with immense vigor. As soon as one made the movement of crouching, she crouched too, but she was always the first to spring, her body upright and her arms wide open, bursting with laughter. She chewed grass, which means thirst. I had a tin of milk opened and she drank it all by the side of the road as noisily as a dog; then she started playing again. She went to piss in the vineyard and wanted to climb into the rooms over the garage by the wall. She kept spitting at Moune. "Madame Moune is nervous," said Jouve, who knows how to treat animals, by the way. With me it was all right at once, barring a certain antagonism, to be sure. But how terribly strong she is already! She is used to the car, and how I wish you had seen her get into it again, with her two adoring maids! She lies in the same room as they do, and if she is left alone, she roars; once she is bedded down for the night, she becomes affectionate, relaxed, and good. She is spotlessly clean. In her car she played through the open window, bit me and gave me her wonderful paws, and spat gently. But she attacks anything that runs or goes on wheels, unhesitatingly. If you had been here, nothing else would have counted for you. Would you like us to go and see her? She lives at Jouve's place, near Aix. Is that on our road? Having such a creature, loving it, would mean taking the veil. One would have to withdraw from the world. . . .

"Barring a certain antagonism, to be sure . . ." More than once I have seen the resistance that some animals have put up against Colette. The word "enmity" would be too strong: it was rather a question of a feeling of competition, as though on the far side of the human person the beast sensed too considerable an animal nature to be overlooked. Colette made no mistake about it; in this reserve she saw a mark of respect and she did not try to make the creature change its attitude. On the other hand, if an animal yielded itself to her, the possession was immediate, entire, and forever.

A little letter found in yesterday evening's post! It was quite delightful. Then we went to the fair, and there we—Véra and I—listened to a huckster for three quarters of an hour. What a great artist. I could have listened to him all day long. A man of the South. A marvel of subtleness, insolence, and servility, as sensitive as a divining rod. He sold all sorts of things, and he knew how to bowl over a coarse-grained housewife by giving her presents—six spoons, four forks. "Isn't that enough, eh? Here are four more, then." And a mind proportioned to that of the crowd. And a deep-bellied car and trunks filled with an incredible, *calculated* chaos of braces, spoons and forks, strong, coarsely woven cloth, velvet cushions, Turkish towels for *six sous,* handkerchiefs at *two* francs a dozen (and he pretended to blow his nose before he sold them), apron strings and braid at a franc for forty meters, and three-franc watches—it all had an intoxicating air of loot. I wanted to ask his name and address, but I did not like to. A jolly Raimu, and intelligent. Such delicacy of touch! A woman said to me, "I have been listening to him since the beginning of the afternoon [it was half past six], and he has not repeated himself once." . . . As we were going home, we saw him again after he had finished; by nature he was a big, melancholy man, a Roman emperor off his pedestal.

Where did it go, that magnificent storm that was hanging over us an hour ago? I swear to you, my dear, that no one knows. It is an absurd country where storms just fade away without anybody seeing them go off. This storm has brought us back the heat in its full strength. It is scarcely nine o'clock: I have done something towards cleaning up the path to the sea, but I am waiting for you for the heavy work. What an utterly still night! Yesterday afternoon at half past six the heat quite emptied the port. And at seven, as though it came through a suddenly kicked-open door, the coolness arrived. (The tomcats are fighting under the window. More cry than wool.)

Sweetheart, this is lovely weather. How can I describe it? It would have to be written down in music.

Who could possibly convey all this freshness, heat, and scented air? It seems to me that all I have written about this country hitherto is mere stuff. My right hand is no use for writing this morning; it has done so many other things already! I have just sent you a wire.

Souci is in a coma. She is, I promise you. She limps with both her front feet, she looks at me as though she had made a mess in the drawing room, and she is hunchbacked. All this because you are not here. What if I did the same? . . .

I am going to nibble at my post—rather behind time—and then we shall go back to the fair, which will be at its height today. No doubt I will come back with a spade stuffed into my bosom and a hoe in my hair. But what I really intend to get is flowerpots.

. . . A full moon over a calm sea: so much so that you feel like saying, "If it is for me, spread it a little less thick."

What is left . . . is the sea, swimming, flowers, walking by myself, and your not being here. An explosion of pink lilies: twenty-nine stems on one side and twenty on the other, in two rows that have flowered at the same time, and each stem has from three to six flowers. It is magnificent. Against the open brickwork wall—you know the wall I mean, the one the tool shed leans against?—another explosion of pink lilies, mixed with a cascade of pale blue plumbago and rivulets of brilliant blue convolvulus. And you are not here!

Pilule [a little she-cat], whom you thought "backward," is an astonishing creature. She bites everything and everybody, swears, grows but little, and leaps like a flea from the ground on to the highest armchairs. She wants meat and fish only, not a drop of milk.

. . . Dédé [André Dunoyer de Segonzac, who was working on the illustrations for *La Treille muscate* in the garden itself—hence the perfect harmony between the text and the pictures in that wonderful book] is working by my side, and he sends you all sorts of affectionate greetings. He is in a state of peaceful fury because his particular Larnac [Larnac had recently brought out an essay on Colette] has just published a *Segonzac*. But his Larnac comes it a bit strong. Dédé was not even told about it beforehand. . . .

We are all of us, quadrupeds and bipeds, on the little terrace. Segonzac silently draws a fuchsia, a little cat, a big cat, me, a bulldog bitch, a pink lily. My dear, I think I shall leave about the twentieth, and by train. Brisson has written me what he calls a despairing letter, begging me to let him have "all that I can" by the twentieth and not a moment later. [Pierre Brisson was waiting for the text of *La Seconde* to publish it in *Les Annales*.] It gives me a bellyache.

. . . At eight o'clock this morning I was in the Borély wood, and it was so lovely there, sea and pine trees and air, that I wept for you with all my soul. But of course I have a soul! Then I raked my Sisyphus copse, where the wind scattered everything as I heaped it up. And Chatte played at being an eel between the teeth of the rake. My writing may look odd: I am sitting here without my spectacles because of the painter who is at work.

I have come back from the hill path filled to overflowing with smells. The milk and hay of the fig trees, the apple and pineapple of the syllium, the sea, the myrtles in flower, the pines, the cistuses, the rosemary . . . Oh, do come soon!

I am making God's own din in the house as I wait for you. Everything that is in the cupboards—blankets, pillows, sheets—gets flung out into the garden. Oh!
. . . There are two splendid melons in the garden that I shall be forced to eat without you: it is quite dreadful. My charming Chatte is in such a state that I have to get out by stealth or she would bruise and wound her tender paws following me. And you will see how delightful it is when I call out in the morning, "All cats for a walk!" Lord above, how strongly everything lives in this country. Everything, including my love for you . . .

. . . So I went for a walk this morning . . . The whole world was quivering with dew; the meadows had the look of hoarfrost; the sea was green and pink. And as I have never stayed here so long, I did not know this particular lighting and this lowness of the sun in the sky. In front of the Espinasse building site, a pretty three-colored cat, not at all thin, sat gazing straight in front of itself at the landscape.

. . . Found a little gecko on the bars, a finger-sized marvel, striped all over like a tabby cat, and the same color. The creatures are changing too. There are quantities of big praying mantises: yesterday evening there was a huge one, a refreshing green. And each time I reached out my hand, he raised one of his clawlike front legs—"Take care," with a face and indeed an expression that surprised me.

. . . This morning under the stormy clouds and over Les Salins there were five or six waterspouts. Alas, I did not see the finest one, but Julio and Eva Dumesnil saw it quite close, at Les Salins, and they fled. A real waterspout, you know, the kind that is like a diabolo running along upright. sucking up the sea and finally collapsing in a dreadful bubbly turmoil— the two witnesses saw it perfectly. Four, five more came after it, and Véra came to tell me to climb on to the flatroof. I will tell you just how splendid it was later.

No news, my dear. The mistral died away yesterday evening, leaving us astonished in the middle of unequaled silence. Even the acacia leaves are motionless. But the flies are madly active.

Yesterday a band of very young swallows took shelter on the wires over the kitchen door; it was so hard for them to hang on with their little claws that every now and again one would cry out in distress. And after nightfall the goldfinches, who had not been able to eat all day, were chirping as they pecked about in the sunflowers.

. . . I have already been pulling things up: all the flowers are over except the violet asters, which make an immense cloud, in the middle of which chance and autumn's taste have set a few flame-colored cannas and —do try to imagine it—above it all the long-lasting blue morning glory! It is a shock to your eyes—one that gives a piercing delight. All the more so since the fine weather, which has come back, has returned to its September state. Raked the patio, *ran* beside the sea— for this year, my dear, *I run!* My speed does not really put Ladoumègue in danger, but I can go through the motions of running and that fills me with a happy astonishment.

. . . But leaving that aside, I do not see how my letters could be less than six pages every day. Late yesterday afternoon I was in the town with Moune [Hélène Jourdan-Morhange] and Kessel [Georges, Joseph Kessel's brother], with time to collect the half past six post and to go to the little shop [it sold cosmetics that Colette manufactured at one time] and see Jeanne Marnac, who was to be there having her nails done. I was buying something at Vachon's when two hands blindfolded me and a pleasant weight pressed against my back. It was Missia [Sert], full of affection. Gushings: loving words. "What, are you here?" "Yes, indeed, I'm here," etc. But she had something urgent for my ear. "She's going to marry him, you know!" "Who?" "Iribe [well-known artist and designer who helped create the 1925 style]. Darr-ling, darr-ling, it's absolutely amazing—Coco [Chanel] is in love for the first time in her life." Comments, views, remarks. "Oh, that fellow certainly knows his trade, I promise you!" I did not have time to ask what trade. "We have been looking for

you. We went to your house: we are going to take you
to have dinner at Saint-Raphaël, at Cannes, at . . ."
I refuse, I plunge into her arms again. I leave with
Moune and we go to recover Kessel, who was buying
everything that came to hand. Three steps later, and
two arms were clasped about me: it was Bernstein's
Gazelle [Henri Bernstein's wife] and her daughter.
Gushings, etc. "We have been looking for you; we are
going to take you to have dinner at Robert de Rothschild's at Valescure . . ." etc. She already knew I was
taking on the [theatrical] criticism for *Le Journal*.
More gushing: kisses. Moune and I set off once more.
Three steps; two reaping arms (belonging to Faucheur
[reaper]—Magnan). It was the Fauchier-Magnans: "I
have just come from your house; I have been looking
for you; I am going to take you to dinner at L'Escale
with . . ." etc. . . . I turn it down at first glance, and
no nonsense about it. Once more we set off, Moune
and I; we make three steps, and two very slim cool
hands close over my eyes: it is Coco Chanel. Gushings
. . . but more restrained. "I am going to take you to
dinner at L'Escale . . ." etc., etc. I refuse more and
more firmly, and a few paces away I see Iribe blowing
me kisses. Then before I can go through the motions
of exorcism he embraces me and squeezes my hand
tenderly between his cheek and his shoulder. "How
dreadfully unkind you have been to me . . . You
called me a fiend!" "Wasn't that good enough for
you?" I said. But he was brimming over with joy and
affection. Altogether he numbers sixty years and twenty
springs. He is thin, wrinkled, and white, and when he
laughs he shows his brand-new teeth. He coos like a
dove, which by the way is rather strange, for in the old

texts you will find that the fiend takes on the voice and the shape of Venus' bird.

(Did you think that was all? Child! A telephone call has just this minute warned me of the arrival of Antoinette Bernstein, the Baroness Robert de Rothschild, and various other rare birds.) Of course, after all that, it was a quarter to eight. Moune was waiting patiently: Kessel had run aground on a breakwater . . .

Anything more, God forbid? Absolutely nothing more today, not a single line, for these ladies and gents are coming and my feet are dreadful [Colette wore nothing but sandals] and I have ancient working clothes on. The men here have gone off fishing. I shall not be surprised if the smell of frying rabbit, this evening or tomorrow morning, betrays the success of their venture.

When I received this letter, was I as aware of its intense vitality as I am today? Probably not, for I knew the people in it far too well and I was too much part of what was going on. Among Colette's gifts, there was that of a great portraitist. When you come to think of it, how could it have been otherwise? Did not the miracles of Colette as a writer consist of the union in one person of an unrivaled power of observation, a steady determination to show us exactly what she had herself thought out, and a most unusual talent for doing so? Scattered here and there in her work are a certain number of remarkable snapshots. I collected them into a little volume called *Trait pour trait;* and again in the posthumous *Paysages et Portraits*. For anyone who knew him, the sketch of Paul Iribe deserves to be included in the collection. Few French writers have set themselves to portraiture. The masters are still Cardinal de Retz, with his sequence of seventeen, and Saint-Simon, whose unfailing eye provided him with the matter and his bitterness with the sharper strokes.

It is clear to what a degree the quiet little port of our first holidays was changing into a branch of the Ritz, well before it welcomed Montparnasse and then later Saint-Germain-des-Près. Soon, going to see Colette became one of the attractions of the place, even for people who did not know her. They came by land and by sea, and they were to be found lying in ambush in the garden. The persecution grew worse and worse, and in the end Colette was left with only one solution—to sell. This she did in 1938.

. . . So there you are, grappling with a new trade [I was going to the rehearsals of one of J. B. Priestly's plays, the French adaptation of which I had written] and commonplace actors, not one of whom is modest. I have repeated your crack about Pitoëff, and it has had the utmost success. And who is this Ursula you think so much of? I am snapping my jaws already, and sharpening my hedge-trimming shears!

. . . I have nothing to tell you, and you know that always takes at least two pages. Did no work yesterday, because of having the Lombards, the Lucs, and Leba to lunch, and because of Géraldy, who came, borne on that breath of wind that makes El Greco's draperies so rounded and theatrical (I may sell Albert Flament that phrase for at least three francs). He was just back from Paris, where, between trains, he was going to see Willemetz. Between trains he read *Duo* [a play Paul Géraldy had based on Colette's novel] to him; between trains he cleverly turned Wille[metz] into a kind of manager for the play. Between trains he was told—you can see my delight—that the end of his third act was no good at all. It was almost dark when he went off.

. . . My dear, I am writing to you early because I am letting myself be dragged off to a picnic by my neighbors. For us women, it is merely a question of carrying the food by car to the creek where the men will land. That is not beyond my strength. The men will haul up their lines and with proud cries wave one *girelle* and two little *pageots,* and with the gravity of Boy Scouts they will cook them on the beach. They put to sea tonight at eleven o'clock to lay out their lines, and we women—a poor, chief-less squaw was I— waited up there on the terrace, ready to brandish the well-filled goblets . . .

I went to see the Émile Ollivier villa at Beauvallon. Oh, how beautiful, how Second Empire, how gently sloping, shaded with magnificent plane trees, huge eucalyptuses, persimmons! What lovely ancient cellars, with wine cisterns so huge they are built into the very walls and it is the wall that jets the wine, in an unexpected and most luxurious fashion. And it will end up as a hotel, like all the others. Such a pity.

Five persons, of both sexes, were waiting for me, sitting outside on my little low wall. They had asked Pauline if they might see me come in. How revolting. I had left the bitches here, and I have been seized upon and welcomed quite terribly. By way of a loving punishment, Souci almost devoured me.

These five people were only the silent vanguard of a band that presently grew bolder, brandishing cameras and books to be autographed.

. . . I am writing again to tell you . . . that I am not in plaster any more. You are utterly amazed: so am I. I summoned Frichement [physician at Saint-Tropez] to ask him to ease my lot, for it was hurting me so in two places that I could not bear it any longer. He looked, plunged in grave reflection, and decided: "Come, we'll do away with the whole thing!" Then there began an Inquisition scene that would have filmed charmingly. Frichement in a nightshirt to his middle, sweating to cut through an unconquerable plaster with specially designed scissors that would not cut, and then with a hunting knife and our three secateurs! I held my leg and laughed and laughed. Finally it ended with a sculptural group—Frichement on one side, tugging at a plaster shell, and Pauline on the other, as though they were opening one of those enormous tropical mollusks. Don't worry: I was neither shaken nor hurt . . .

141 ❀

It was at the beginning of September, in 1931, that
Colette broke her fibula; and I was there at the time.
This is how it happened, this accident that I should
call stupid if it were not for the fact that all accidents
are stupid. We had decided to go and bathe at Les
Salins, about a mile from La Treille muscate. There
was a road to this beach, and it ended in a footpath: I
drove the car a little too far along the path. "I'll turn
now," I said to Colette, "so that we shall not have to
do it in the heat of the day, after we have swum." But
to make things easier, she had already jumped out and
run to an iron gate that opened on to a property along
the road. Or I should say, one that was supposed to
open, for it did not. As she stepped back, Colette did
not notice one of those very narrow ditches, at least
three feet deep, that they scoop out so dangerously in
the South—ditches which are made practically invisible by the grass in the summer and which seem quite
pointless to those who have not undergone the pelting
autumnal rains of Provence. Her right leg plunged
straight down into it, and her heel struck heavily
against the hard bottom, while she herself fell over on
the road. She began to scream. Souci, the bulldog,
leapt out of the door and raced towards her. I was sure
that Colette had broken something, and in order to be
able to hurry her off without losing a second, I re-
versed furiously so as to get the wretched car round at

last: but in my confusion I put a wheel into the ditch, and nothing, nothing could get it out.

Even now, I blame myself for this lack of calmness in an emergency: that is the sort of thing that true remorse is made of. In announcing that "we all have enough fortitude to bear the woes of others," M. de La Rochefoucauld only made it clear that he had never loved; he also justified Cardinal de Retz's hesitant remark in his portrait: "There has always been something outside my comprehension throughout M. de La Rochefoucauld."

I ran to the beach and called Luc-Albert Moreau and Hélène Jourdan-Morhange, who happened to be there. With the utmost care we put Colette into their car. Five minutes later she was home, imperatively calling for something to eat—a healthy reaction of hers that I have noticed in all circumstances, even the most dramatic.

The doctor did in fact detect a broken bone, and he at once telephoned the hospital, the only place that possessed an X-ray apparatus (the most archaic that can be imagined), and called for an ambulance. At the mere word "hospital," Louise and Lamponi, the two caretakers, and the other local women who had hurried up, covered their faces. With dismay all over her countenance, Louise moved away, murmuring, "The hospital! What a disgrace: what a disgrace for us!" The fact that the ambulance was the municipal ambulance, which would have just as willingly gone out to pick up a run-over tramp, was the crowning humiliation for them. One blunder more and they would have put on mourning.

The break was clean and the bone knit well. But still it is likely that the violent blow on the heel, transmitted to her hip, caused some very slight degree of damage there that allowed the arthritis to get a hold at that point some years later.

. . . It is very hard for me to write in the company of a cat that wants to get *into* my fountain pen.

. . . My dinner yesterday was very splendid. L'Escale provided me with stuffed bass and a dish of partridges with cabbage, bacon, and sausages that amazed the Vanders. To drink, cup made with Alsatian wine, light and very good. (Oh, half-witted creature, not to be here!) It was a lovely Saturday. A dense crowd; a warm evening; Gotha in overalls. A much-titled fairy in a khaki cotton blouse and a laborer's belt. "Fashionable" women in cheap men's shirts. Fernande C. in an evening frock, with jewels, and her hair lacquered: a mug like a butcher run to fat. She had immense jade beads on her arms and round her neck, and a bosom-showing gigolo in a yellow and brown sweater, a tall, wizened marmoset with shaved eyebrows painted on again, a sharp peak of hair on his forehead like a Mary Stuart cap, and the same peak going down the nape of his neck. Most surprising.

From a table full of women dressed as boys, and

men with huge scarves, there arose a tall bony old hag clad in a nineteen-franc pair of blue canvas breeches and a tiny striped cotton sailor's singlet. The heavily made-up face of a domestic servant out of a job, a sweet little beret perched on the dyed locks. It came up to me and said, "How glad I am to see you again!" As you can imagine, I did not utter a word. It added: "We haven't seen one another since that evening at Madame de——'s." Confronted with my look of a dull-witted hedgehog, she told me her name. . . . How you would have laughed. These ladies danced together afterwards, smoking as they danced, and the said princess whistled at the table. They danced as nobody would dare dance in the rue Blomet. The Negresses in the rue Blomet do have some sort of restraint.

So I saw a thousand head of cattle. At about eleven o'clock I even beheld the arrival, with a man, of a poor reduced flattened creature with a provocative Panama hat and a face so ravaged that it wounded and frightened one—Madame ——; she was looking for a table. She was altered beyond recognition, but I am sure it was she. She saw me; she said something to her husband; they pretended not to be able to find a table and they left. It is very curious, the way nothing whatever is left of that woman who was a piece of scenery, something always built up over an intellectual void. Logical enough: but still surprising. The man is her husband.

I have not been able to resist reproducing this little picture, this etching, this page worthy of Goya's Caprichos. It was so unusual for Colette to let her

caustic humor have its head! There are only a few
pages in *Chéri* that give a hint of what she might have
done in satire; for forbearance does not mean blind-
ness. Nothing could prevent her seeing people, even
her friends, just as they were. This was why she always
declined to pass judgment on her contemporaries in
interviews or at other times. These lines were for my
amusement alone, and it would be a serious betrayal
of Colette to quote the names that occur in them.
Anyway, by now they would not convey much to most
people. Again, do we not take a lively pleasure in
reading some memoirs, such as those of Tallemant des
Réaux or Vieil-Castel, for their savagery even now
that the victims' names no longer mean anything to
us?

Julio came back half an hour after midnight: he had
been fish-spearing without a spear, but they did bring
back some splendid full-flavored sea urchins. At night
the urchins leave their rocks and graze on the seaweed,
and all you have to do is to gather them in a net while
they feed. Even here fishing has its surprises: in the
market the day before yesterday there was an angel
shark, as big as a man and as ugly as a devil.

Yesterday evening, the sudden fall of night in the
suddenly forsaken little port. Everything changed:
L'Escale empty, Sénéquier's with few people in it, and
Kismet full. In a few days I hope you will be able to

spend an hour or so in the nocturnal Saint-Tropez of earlier days, with almost all its charm. The light at breakfast this morning, a spreading silver-blue; flowers; Chatte luxuriating on her cushion, smiling vaguely; a temperature like that in one's dreams of flying—you really, really ought to have been here.

I have picked these familiar scenes, these quickly drawn landscapes, almost by chance out of some four hundred letters. Colette and I lived together so easily that you may believe me when I assert that they are entirely devoid of any anxiety about their literary aspects. That, in my opinion, is what makes them so valuable. They help me to bring you back to life, O light-filled days and scented nights of Saint-Tropez. It may be an illusion, but it seems to me that the older I grow, the more brilliant my memories become. Perhaps because I have painfully learned not to tarnish them with regret. Regret for what we have lost is, like sorrow, a natural emotion; but we also think of it as an obligation. We consider it a profanation to fight against it, and right behavior to encourage it. In my view this is a mistaken idea of real devotion. To regret is to lose all over again. One ought, on the contrary, to give the happy days one has lived every possible chance of retaining their radiance and acquiring a second reality. Tears only make them fade and threaten them with destruction, whereas joy does them honor. Happiness in living is not enough for me: I also need that of having lived.

When she was questioned about happiness, Colette replied, "Happiness? Come, what should I do with it?" And sometimes, "Happiness? I haven't the time for it."

Badgered by questioners of every shape and size, she generally escaped them by quips and flashes of wit. "What do you think, madame, about . . . ?" "I write, monsieur; do I have to think too?" One day she was asked to quote the most beautiful love letter she knew, and if necessary to compose a hypothetical one herself. She answered, "The key will be under the mat tonight." As for happiness, I am not sure that if she had reflected, her answer would have been any different. For her, not having the time did not mean being overburdened with work. Even during the quite rare periods when she was not writing, she was too busy to give herself up to general ideas, to intellectual speculation. Busy at what? At living: just that. And, for her, living primarily meant exercising her tireless curiosity. I was going to write *satisfying,* but that would not have been the right word, for of its very nature curiosity never can be satisfied. Hers less than anybody else's, since when she thought about the beings and the objects within her immediate range, they always seemed new and fresh to her. Who has not wanted to write, to paint—in short, to create? In this context, I am not talking about those declared vocations that will last, that will endure. I am thinking of all of us who do not manage to live fully enough to "unrepress" ourselves completely and who retain within us the remaining dregs of something unexpressed, unsatisfied, unfulfilled. In this respect Colette had nothing whatever to impel her towards writing. In the same way, I never spoke to her about what I call winged breathing, for I was afraid that she might not understand that I, even in the very midst of the happiness that we were living together, still needed to assuage a dull emptiness that was part and parcel of my state as an ordinary man.

Later, much later, when she found herself gradually deprived of movement by the arthritis in her hip, Colette devoted long, meditative hours to tapestry work. I was often with her, and we said very little to one another: we loved that trustful silence between us, a quietness based upon an affection that had no need to proclaim itself. Did her thoughts then leave earthly cares, and was she then concerned with metaphysical speculation? I can only say that she never spoke to me about any such thing, even in the lucid hours of her final illness. Male presumption would have me add: "She would certainly have told me about it." But, in such an important matter, honesty compels me to state, on the contrary, that although we were united in our life together as few couples have ever been, we always, both of us, respected the other's privacy.

People often say to me, "You who lived thirty years with Colette, you can tell us whether it is not very difficult, if not impossible, to share one's daily bread with a genius." I must add that it is usually Anglo-Saxons who ask me this question, because for them genius and chaos are much more than a mere association of words. A little while ago, vexed by a rather nagging kind of woman journalist, I let myself go and replied, "I do not know, madame. Ask my wife." The best of it was that she did not look upon this as face-tiousness, but rather as revenge that I was trying to take upon the woman whose brilliant fame put me so entirely in the shade.

I have never met a more natural woman than Colette. I do not deny that some works owe their strength and their particular quality to a streak of madness in their creators; but the artists whose success arises from such a streak nevertheless form a very small minority indeed. In the writers of the first rank whom I have had the good fortune to meet I have found one quality common to all—humility before their work. And this self-doubt necessarily leads to simplicity. Only the commonplace are tempted to give themselves the airs of inspiration, to put on temperament and to play the domestic tyrant on the grounds of their extreme sensitivity. Furthermore, the Latin sense of balance does not willingly go in for this sort of thing. If Coppet echoes with the quarrels between Benjamin Constant and Madame de Staël and if in the end the squabbling reached such a pitch that Benjamin dragged his mistress painstakingly up and down the stairs by the hair, it only proves that both the one and the other dearly loved the domestic scene.

Seen from the outside, Colette's life seems to be full

of extravagant flights: her behavior often astonished people and sometimes shocked them. The truth is that she had inherited a high degree of independent judgment from Sido, her mother. She nevertheless obeyed a private code of very severe laws governing conduct; but they did not always coincide with current morality. Neither did her scale of values. Above all, she made the distinction between work that was well done and work that was not, without holding that there were some callings more honorable than others. "What was wrong with me appearing in the music halls, providing I did it conscientiously, or with making cosmetics, so long as my recipes were good ones?"

She made up her mind very quickly—this was another aspect of her spontaneity, or perhaps its fruit— and she had a high degree of impatience. And yet for more than fifty years she obliged herself to write several hours a day without leaving her "workbench"— crossing out, beginning again, never leaving the smallest sentence that did not satisfy both her ear and her elevated notion of her professional duty.

She brought the same gifts and the same virtues to her housekeeping. She could not have prevented herself from doing so, even if she had wanted to. For Sido, at the same time that she handed on her highly personal way of looking at things, had also transmitted a whole range of peasant wisdom, the love of well-stocked cupboards and sweet-smelling linen, the art of making a fire and of keeping it up, the secret of dishes cooked for long hours under the ashes, a hundred little skills, a thousand recipes.

It was only when the top was screwed back on her fountain pen that she rewarded herself for the long immobility that her work had forced upon her. Then she literally exploded into activity. Until arthritis rather than age slowed the rhythm of her life, she lived it at a furious pace. "Quick, quick," was the word her household heard more often than any other. Naturally I too found myself caught up in this whirl. I was very far from being against it: on the contrary, the sight of this splendid releasing of energy rejoiced my heart.

"But still," people say to me, "you had a very strong personality to deal with, and if you had been equally assertive, there would have been dreadful clashes." The underlying meaning of these words is clear enough. In a pair it must be the man who, even if he is wholly wrong, imposes his tastes, his notions, and his arbitrary views. Perpetually giving way to his partner and making himself inconspicuous in her wake is beneath his dignity.

For my part, I think that one has to be very strangely wanting in love to let it take second place to personal vanity, and that one must be strangely wanting in value not to recognize a greater value in another. If manliness consists of throwing out one's chest and strutting about like a farmyard cock, I do not think very much of it. I feel that a man cannot have a nobler task than that of serving a country, a cause, an idea, or a great destiny. And if he must sacrifice his own hopes and ambitions to this service, then he will do so with the utmost joy.

I am quite willing to believe that the part I played beside Colette had no precedent. That was one motive more for undertaking it. To be sure, I have sometimes been called Monsieur Colette: I should have thought it contemptible in me to take offense.

She and I knew that for a relationship to last there must necessarily be a continual watchfulness—it cannot bear carelessness. We each had a part to play in insuring the lasting success of ours. My part called for the help of that most unsure of auxiliaries—time.

Colette was gay and impetuous: she nevertheless harbored a deep pessimism, and for a long while this could be seen showing through her work, clear to anyone who looked at it attentively. She was rather scornful of her fame, and she did not wholly believe in it;

and of her past life she remembered the failures and unhappinesses above all other things. The enchanted gardens of her childhood and her happy bringing-up under the incomparable Sido's wing could not make her forget that that Eden had been violently destroyed and that nest trodden underfoot. Colette was sixteen when Sido was ruined by Juliette, her daughter by her first marriage, and by the family of Juliette's husband—a tortuous peasant conspiracy, dark, crooked machinations, so that not only did the last, smallest patch of land have to be sold, but even the furniture had to be put up for auction. The whole family had to leave Saint-Sauveur and its woods and go to Châtillon-Coligny in the Loiret, where they took refuge in a very small house provided by the generosity of Achille, her faithful, beloved half-brother. Colette recovered from the pathological listlessness that this shock caused, but the bitter remembrance of it stayed with her.

Her experiences of marriage, too, had not been happy, so that she no longer believed in love as anything but a brief flame that must soon die away, leaving only ashes behind it.

I set myself gently by the side of this woman whom life had so wounded, and I did so with the firm determination of proving to her that fidelity was not an empty word. Year by year she grew more persuaded of this, and her last books bear witness to a serenity that she would not otherwise have acquired.

The question of a religious funeral had never come up between us, and it was not because of any wish expressed by Colette that I, having sought my friends' advice, asked that she should be buried with the rites of the Church. But the sudden stunning silence of death does not entirely break the bond between two who have been so close to one another. I knew very well that Colette would have approved of the step I was taking. France is a Catholic country; her history and that of Catholicism march together, even when she abjured it during the Revolution; and France's national funerals take place in Notre Dame. Hence, once you have been baptized, and if, like Colette, you are not outside the pale of the Church, the fact of not asking for a religious burial is not merely an abstention. It becomes a positive act, one that displays not mere indifference but active hostility. Although she often spoke roughly, Colette was the most courteous person imaginable, and she would have regarded it in the first place as a piece of incivility. Like not leaving a card at the French embassy when you are staying in a foreign capital.

How would she have received the refusal I met with? Certainly with the humility that she always showed and that is at least a Christian virtue. She used still to dream that she was going in for her lower certificate of education and that she failed. "I have not passed my final examination," she would have thought, quite simply. But had she really been examined? In any case, she would have been less surprised by this repulse than by the strong feelings it aroused in the Catholic world—an emotion whose echoes still reach me from time to time.

I shall not plead for her any more than she would have pleaded for herself. I keep my protest solely for those who at that time accused Colette of anticlericalism. I challenge them to find a single word in her books against the clergy or even against religion. But her accusers would have it that her very silence was in itself significant; it must mean that she opposed religion. It was impossible to know Colette even slightly without being aware that she did not display systematic opposition to anything at all.

To be sure, she was not a believer. Neither Sido nor the captain had ever provided her with an example; nor had anyone else in her later life. Yet she was by no means one who would turn others away from the faith. I will not go so far as to say that she aroused vocations in those about her, but it is a striking fact that two young women who lived very much with her were converted—Claude Chauvière and Renée Hamon.

Claude Chauvière was Colette's secretary for two years. She wrote several books that are not without merit; and one of them is called *Colette*. She was rather short, with extremely beautiful eyes the color of the Breton sea: I did not know her well, and I was not in a position to follow the stages of her return to religion. Colette agreed to be the godmother at her christening. I think she hoped to become a nun: there again I do not know what obstacles barred her path. One day in summer we went, Colette and I, to Angers, when Claude Chauvière was going through some kind of preparatory stage at the Franciscan convent of L'Esvière. I remember a delightful garden, in which I should not have been—a garden whose antiquity was vouched for by its enormous trees. I remember a blue and lunar evening, an incomparable silence. In the middle of the park, a very small chapel, into which we furtively peered. By the light of the candles we could make out two kneeling nuns, their immobility heightened by their white veils and scarlet-trained habits. In that place prayer never stops, day or night.

Colette's letters to Claude Chauvière still exist, but

I have not yet managed to see them. I believe that they would tell us more about Colette's attitude towards those who are touched by grace. When she was writing to Renée Hamon's "best friend" when Renée was at the point of death, she said, "She has nuns around her, and they are teaching her to pray, she says. Those are good people to be with, and the murmur of prayers is a good, gentle sound . . ."

Indeed, for a certain time it might have been thought that Colette was leaning in the direction of religion. François Mauriac, the most subtle of guides, was showing her the path. During the war—in 1943, if I am not mistaken—there was a kind of spiritual flirtation between them. At that time Mauriac came to see Colette quite often. Although their attitudes were so unlike, they valued one another highly. Colette had thought a great deal of him ever since his first books, and she had urged me to read *Le Désert de l'amour*, *Le Noeud de vipères* and *Thérèse Desqueyroux* at a time when she and I were only at the stage of confidences. I shared her liking, being moved, as she was, by that whispered passion, that sensuality which was all the more ardent for knowing itself guilty, and that hot breath with its aftertaste of brimstone. Today Mauriac as a person, as a vigorous journalist with a dialectic that delights some and infuriates others, has grown to such a size that his novels are somewhat overshadowed. Mauriac is eclipsing Mauriac.

For his part, François Mauriac was never mistaken about Colette and the importance of her work; all he tried to do was to draw her towards the shores he himself frequented, by calling her a moral writer of immoral themes. But whatever it was, praise or blame, everything that Mauriac wrote about Colette delighted her. " 'What flower has she left unvisited, this splendid bee?' " she often quoted.

The man enchanted her; but whom does Mauriac not enchant, if once he set his mind to it? What a perfect emissary the Evil One would have had in him, if only he had not been so immovably attached to the other side of the barrier. With his head slightly thrown back, his Adam's apple showing, his eyes screwed up, distilling urbanity, he would come into the room where Colette was waiting for him on her couch, surrounded by the emblems of her private fairyland, chilly even in the height of summer, cordial and intimadating. Their dialogue would begin. Mauriac's breath was short and his voice a wreck, but this he turned into an additional charm, for it caused his words to seem to be very carefully made for the use of his listener alone.

Very soon, led by this most practiced hand, Colette,

whether she was aware of it or not, found herself turning to unfamiliar pursuits. Presently, to my great surprise, I saw her reading the Bible, Saint Paul's Epistles, and other religious books.

Each of us carries about with him the aura that his most deeply rooted thought has brought into being. Colette would cause cats to appear in places where it would have seemed that no cat could possibly be. If Carco took a walk by night, a battle between knife-bearing thugs would materialize before him. Minor miracles preceded or followed Mauriac's visits. A whole set of coincidences built themselves up around a black missal that Colette remembered from her childhood, and it was hard not to believe that a supernatural hand had chosen to show itself. Mauriac has given an account of this strange business himself, so I shall certainly not attempt it myself.

I know that Mauriac, encouraged by this sign, thinks that he was very close indeed to bringing Colette to God. I am of a different opinion, and I should give my reasons if I were not afraid of entering into conflict with so formidable an adversary. I only grant him the fact that for a while Colette paid particular attention to religious history, symbols, and ceremonies—subjects that were never entirely outside the range of her curiosity, after all.

Paradoxically, it was I who became the victim, or if you prefer, the beneficiary, of this atmosphere: Colette asked Mauriac to help her in bringing about my conversion. Her motives for this were many and various, but no doubt the strongest was the hope (the vain hope) that at this moment when she knew I was in great danger I might gain some degree of immunity from being a Christian. Who can blame her? As for me, I did not wish to refuse to take a step that Colette urged upon me if it could provide her with the slightest ease of mind at a period that was particularly grudging in such comforts. Furthermore, I do not feel myself set apart from the Church by anything except the feeling that she cannot accept my heterodox notion of God.

My mind has always been concerned with the search for a higher being; but it has never been granted me either to achieve faith or to feel really deprived of it. Sometimes I have been so allured by the Christian discipline that I have been tempted to join it. Not in order to abjure the Judaism to which I belong, but because, like Bergson, I feel that Christianity is its "modern edition." When I am tired of holding up the spiritual world that I have fashioned for myself—a weary, solitary Atlas—and when I long for the props that an already thought-out religion would give me, I think of the one I have met on every page of France's history, the religion which by its bulls, its councils, and its policy continues to evolve, whereas mine is necessarily static.

At all events, Mauriac arranged an interview for me with a Jesuit, a Father Fessard. This appointment gave rise to a misunderstanding that was so much in line with Mauriac's approach and with what some theologians call "God's humor" that it provides yet another justification of what Colette so often said: "You cannot write anything with impunity."

The meeting was to be at 17, rue Monsieur, and I did not know that this was the Maison des Jésuites. I had written down the address some days before, and I did not check it. At that time I was forbidden to work, and as I had a good deal of time on my hands I spent some of it among the bookshops. My feet led me to that quarter automatically, and as woolgathering is not the least of my faults, at the appointed time I found myself not in the rue Monsieur but in the narrow rue Monsieur-le-Prince, gazing with some concern at a hotel whose appearance filled me with astonishment. I said to myself that no doubt Father Fessard was a country prelate, and so why should he not put up in an unpretentious place on the Left Bank during his brief stays in Paris?

I opened a door, which set a little bell a-ringing, then I crossed a corridor and came face to face with a very well nourished and undoubtedly female form. Her bosom tended to overflow, she was painted to the eyes, and long, pear-shaped earrings swung about her cheeks; in the kindest way, she asked me what she could do to be of service.

"Is Father Fessard staying here, if you please?"

Her reply was so quick that you would have sworn she had it ready: "Father Fessard, no; but we have a little Mother Fessarde who will certainly do your business for you."

I was by no means sure how François Mauriac would take my blunder. He burst into a laugh that hunched up his shoulders, and his hands moved in that well-known turning gesture; he looked at me with his most mischievous twinkle, and in his most relentless tone he breathed out the words, "You are on the right road!"

Alas, I was not. The priest who was good enough to see me, in the rue Monsieur this time, made me understand this quite clearly. I told him that in the first place I wished to belong to the religion of my country out of respect and affection. For me, God was the highest idea of man that I could conceive, a horizon, as it were, that continually receded. And since God had made man in His image, I could not be so very far from the right teaching. Furthermore, I imprudently added, since the essence was still charity and the quest for perfection, did going into the question of whether God created man or man God really matter?

Father Fessard received my words with the utmost coldness: he insisted that I should have a simple unquestioning faith and that I should blindly accept the dogmas. "I know," he ended, "that the conversion of adults is difficult. Pray to God that He may cause you to be touched by His grace."

It was an unambiguous refusal, and one that astonished me for a moment. But a moment later I saw that Father Fessard was right. Regular armies, I told myself, are not wrong to mistrust francs-tireurs even if they are on their side. The Church, whose mission it is to wrest mankind from doubt and to give it hope, must show herself as a single, unbroken rock, of which nothing can be rejected without the risk of losing the whole. The Church may overlook it if a Christian who joined the fold before he could walk happens to soften the dogmas and call what he should accept as truths symbols, so long as he does not make a fuss about it. But the man who comes knocking at the door should do so with the utmost humility. Could I deny that I was only asking asylum for my own convenience, and that, of the props I was asking for, I meant to retain only those I might find agreeable, and none that would be a nuisance—the poetry of the rites, but none of their rigors?

That was how I argued against myself and *pro domo Christi* twenty years ago. I believe that today the priest's answer would not be the same, so far has the Church, feeling that in the near future she will have to spread her wing over all those who do not formally reject her, moved along the road of evolution. Rome, lying there in the world's center, continually shows that it is more clearly aware of the fact that since new times are begetting new unhappinesses, mankind, with the threat of the atomic bomb hanging over it, longs for a common spiritual defense which may overrule all political interests and at last be able to protect man from his fellows.

"Is it possible that Colette's unwavering devotion to all created things should not have pleased the Creator?"

"That is not the point," they told me. "The Church is a body to which one cannot belong without obeying its rules. Oh, if only at the last moment Colette had repented of her errors! If only a priest had been able to make the necessary gesture, even from far off, in the darkness of an anteroom, or through an open door!"

Very well, since I understand nothing of all this.

Yet I should have liked to have a cross on the pink and black granite tomb I made for her at the Père-Lachaise; I should have liked it because of a certain taste I have for harmony, because of a certain idea I have conceived of that glorious sign, and also because of my fear that one day people will no longer be able to make out which it was, the Church or she who lies there, who refused to let the cross be placed over her.

An extreme physical suffering brings with it insensitivity to pain, so the first shock of bereavement possesses a numbing quality. You reach a secondary state in which a kind of heroism takes up its abode in you—you are involved in everything that occurs, but not very deeply involved. I had experienced my greatest distress when it became obvious to me that Colette's end was no more than a question of months, perhaps of days. When she had in fact died, and died in a calm serenity that went beyond my hopes, I felt a sort of relief: she was protected now. Protected from misfortune and the loss of her powers, in the same way that the wonderful adventure that we had lived together was now beyond harm's reach. All was over. The rest was my concern alone.

This is a stage, a relief, that does not last. Presently absence makes itself felt. What is loneliness in comparison with that? Soon this absence is to be found everywhere, at every moment of the day, in every movement and in every thought. When it became too strong for me, I showed no more fortitude than anyone else—I tried to escape from it. I made use of all the alleviations of the weak—drink, night life . . . But there is no worse moment than that at which, in the midst of a spurious excitement, your heart is suddenly wrung and the pain that you thought you had eluded springs up before you, stronger than ever for its rest.

It is hard for one who had always shared everything until then to fight this sort of battle alone—a battle that one may not win, out of mere want of interest in the victory.

Yet I was less to be pitied than some.

It is a wonderful privilege to retain so powerful a link with the one who has left you as that which is formed by the works of a writer, a painter, or a sculptor. For thirty years on end, I had watched Colette at work, watched her most attentively. The books in which her articles and essays were collected, *Prisons et Paradis, La Jumelle noire, Journal à rebours,* and *En pays connu,* had been assembled by both of us, working together. I had spent three years assembling the material for the fifteen thick volumes of her collected works, which were published towards the end of her life and which for the first time showed the public the real size of Colette as a writer; and she and I, working under the same lamp, had corrected the proofs. This collection astonished Colette more than anyone. "Have I really written all that?" she murmured.

When she entrusted me with all her work and its future, she did so with an emotion by no means usual with her; and the occasion was one of those few when our conversation took on a certain solemnity. What a solid embankment against the abyss it was, this imperative task—a task that allowed no sort of weakness. Colette left behind her nothing that had not appeared in one form or another, but in the course of fifty years she had written for so many publications that a fair number of her articles and short pieces had slipped both her memory and mine, and had not been included in the collections that she made of these essays from time to time. Up until now I have had the good fortune to be able to bring out two posthumous books of hers, *Belles saisons* and *Paysages et Portraits,* which include some of her very finest writing; and these have been followed by four volumes of her letters. At the same time I stimulated and encouraged the translation of her works in all languages and entered into contact with research workers and members of universities all over the world, some working on her biography, others studying various aspects of her personality or the mystery of her magical style as subjects for their theses.

In this way I carried on with the task that Colette had left me, working day by day in the flat on the edge of the gardens of the Palais-Royal, in which not a single piece of furniture, not a single ornament had been moved, much less changed. Pauline, who had looked after Colette for forty years, went on looking after me. I did my utmost to prevent any alteration. When sadness threatened to overcome me, I went into "madame's bedroom," the room where we had spent all our evenings together. I sat, as I used to do, on her couch—the couch where I had heard her last sigh—and everything turned to peace within me.

I do not believe in life after death, at least not in the way that the more artless minds understand it, or in the possibility of communicating with the dead. I may have a certain area of mysticism, but I have already spoken of its limits. Yet insofar as the past shapes the present, when two people, because of a long-enduring love and daily interpenetration, have grown so into one another that words are for them no more than an unessential, ornamental pleasure, then there is no breaking-off of the colloquy—a colloquy not with the partner as she was when death took her away, but with the partner as she was when she was filled with the breath of life.

Henceforward my road seemed to be already drawn out for me. I would watch over these works and this house until the end. Once her tomb was built and the book that I owed her as an act of homage written and finished, at the right moment I should have a commemorative plaque set into the wall of the house and I should cause a street to be named after Colette. I should thus remain a man of one single love and one solitary book. An example of faithfulness unimpaired by death, I should gently fade away in the unaltered setting of my married happiness; and on the black slab which bears just these words, *Here lies Colette,* my friends and hers, when I was laid beside her, would add merely this: *Here her "best friend" came to be with her again.*

This lasted until the day I realized that there is no worse insult to life than to work out one's character, one's role, in this way, and to settle the staging of one's exit even to the very lighting effects. For this slow, splendid going down to succeed, it would have been necessary that I too, having acquired the unchanging state to which I vowed our household objects, should become unalterable, and that henceforth nothing in me would ever be modified.

As insidious and persistent as the sea eating away a shore, an uneasiness began to work within me, and for a long while I tried to deceive myself as to its nature. Just as one tries to convince oneself, at the beginning of a fit of dizziness, that it is one's head that is moving and not the surroundings, so I clung desperately to my illusion that I had stopped the passage of time. Yet Colette herself was changing. My work obliged me to plunge deep into all that she had written, and this showed her to me in a light that was no longer so familiar. All these pieces, dashed off in haste, sometimes finished to satisfy the paper's bicycle boy who was waiting in the kitchen, all these things that had seemed merely contingent, written in the sand, took on the solidity of a planned work. Even in the novels, page after page of which I had seen rewritten, I no longer saw the warp and weft but rather the purity of the style and the feeling. The changeable aspect of the work vanished: I was left face to face with the intangible.

We had lived together, almost always gay, frivolous, quietly happy. Colette only withdrew a few working hours a day from the small change of ordinary talk and our little everyday problems; and even then she did not insist upon silence or isolation—she let herself be interrupted quite happily. It was indeed that simple, always approachable woman and none other who had produced Colette's works, that series of books which form a coherent world whose truth and poetry will never perhaps be equaled. She herself had no idea that she was this creative genius, so she did not hide it from me—besides, I was perfectly aware of it. But now my admiration and my zeal for her work were no longer latent, no longer mingled with the everyday trifles of life, and gradually Colette as a writer took precedence over Colette as my affectionate companion. I relied upon the objects that I saw all around me to bring me back to our ordinary life. But they only gave me the last years of it; and presently they were giving me only the hours of our last parting. When, in an opposing movement, my mind dwelt more and more on the younger days of our idyl, the Garden-of-Paradise hours of Saint-Tropez, they emphasized what I had lost, not what was mine forever. I began to suspect that the true, the only place for remembering is in one's mind. Memories, like everything else, have their own particular ebb and flow.

According to the stimuli that he undergoes, the owner of these memories sees them in a different light. And I reached the point of asking myself whether, in order to keep mine alive and supple, I ought not to take them away from the surroundings that were keeping them in such narrow bounds.

Perhaps these doubts would never have occurred to me if at the same time I had not had an upsurge of vitality in myself to deal with. When Colette died, I was sixty-five, and I had mistaken notions about old age. To some extent she was the cause of this, since throughout her last years I led my life at her rhythm. On the one hand, I had never really seen her change— this happens with people who never leave one another for so much as a day. It is now, when for example I see the film that was made in our flat in the Palais-Royal late in her life, that I exclaim, "God above, how she has aged! That's what happens when she leaves me!" On the other hand, I was no longer making the true distinction between her age and mine. If her life should end before mine, I used to say to myself in those days, I shall wait until time finishes the process of wearing me out in my turn. It never even occurred to me that instead of watching my days come to a close I might come to have other interests and know other places: indeed, the thought would have filled me with horror.

It certainly appears that, for a man, sixty-five marks the end of that rather dangerous period which, for want of a better name, is now called his change of life. Once he has weathered this headland, he would generally set off with the wind behind him if only he would believe that he is at the beginning of the happiest stage of his voyage here below and forbid his mind to dwell upon its end. To be sure, the fact of aging cannot be denied; but it does not seem to me to proceed evenly. For the last thirty years I have not had a single migraine, though I suffered much from them in earlier days; and to my surprise I find myself reading the paper without spectacles, whereas ten years ago I could not have done so to save my life. What is more, I have a wisdom tooth coming, strong, firm, and powerful—a tooth, by the way, that I could very well do without.

I had supposed, then, that I was destined to end my days in a long and soothing meditation on my past, in the midst of the objects that would best call it to mind. Defending such a beloved and familiar literary work would be a sufficient occupation for me, and I should keep in touch with only those aspects of the outer world that would be useful for my task. The exhaustion and distress into which Colette's death plunged me at first provided me for some while with the illusion that I should succeed. I scarcely ever left the house. But presently I took to walking up and down, to and fro, round and round. I was seized with ungovernable fits of impatience, a kind of muscular revolt, which obliged me to stay out until dawn: I thought all this was still caused by my unhappiness, but in fact it was nothing of the kind. Night after night I came home at four in the morning and got up again at eight, as fresh and lively as though I had not committed any excesses at all.

I tried to damp down the blaze that was filling me to the gentle glow that my chosen way of life required, but I tried in vain. I was having an attack of energy, as some people have an attack of listlessness. And yet the thought of Colette never left me for an instant. But the wonderful adventure that we had lived through together was taking on a continually more exciting character for me. I was compelled to admit to myself that the hours I passed over in my recollection gave me happiness, whereas, moved by a general notion that sorrow alone was worthy of mourning, sorrow was what I was looking for.

And lastly, did not these books, which had become my rule of life and my substance, all tend wholly in the direction of living? She who had paid such close attention to birth and to the renewal of life, she who was so far from artificiality that it was difficult for her even to conceive of it, how would she have judged the way I was trying to give myself up to stagnation? And every day there was a greater conflict between the overflowing abundance that gave my breath its rhythm and the plan that I had conceived—between my shimmering, happy memories and the motionless surroundings that perpetuated only one moment of them.

Sometimes, but very furtively, I used to grieve that Colette and I had not had a child. When I met Colette, the days of having children were past for her, and occasionally we spoke of this with regret: though indeed I could scarcely see Colette breaking off between two pages of copy to dandle a baby. Now, thinking of this child that we never had, and without troubling about the age it would have reached, I imagined myself guiding its steps, protecting it from all dangers, talking to it for hours about its mother. It was a thought that no doubt formed a link between an ending and a beginning. I suppose, too, that in men the wish for a child (however much he may love it once it is born) is always a more or less intellectual notion, associated with love, or regret, or perhaps ambition. It does not well up from his innermost being, his vitals, as it does in a woman.

One or two of Colette's friends who, if they were

not of her age were at least of mine, gave me to understand that they would be quite willing to share my solitude. In this way we would wear out our remaining days side by side, talking of her we had loved so well. Happily they did not express themselves with such frankness that I was unable to misunderstand. The picture of Colette that these friends had formed had of necessity very little in common with what I myself had experienced, and I should very soon have found the comparison of the two images quite unbearable. I do not know whether they thought that I should leave the flat or whether they would come and settle there with me: I was not ripe for the one, and the other would have led me straight to murder in the first degree.

"We are the same age," one of them told me. Alas, in love women are not the same age as men when they have the same count of years. Yet I dare say they feel the same impulses, the same revivals of energy, the same longings for happiness. If there are delights in growing old for them as there are for us, it is for them to let us know; and I place the title of this book at their disposal.

The years moved by, and I did not move with them. My surroundings, on the other hand, lost their color by imperceptible degrees, and that was something I had never expected at all. Everything faded; a crack appeared in the wallpaper; a piece of furniture lost its finish. How was I to shelter my living past from this process of aging?

I had a friend and neighbor, Madame Laure, a Russian from the Russia of the Tsars and a remarkable woman of whom I have spoken elsewhere: sometimes she came up to see me. She had formerly been rich and now she put up with extreme poverty without seeming to notice it; she had great style, a keenly judging and independent mind. She had positively worshipped Colette, who loved her and knew her value. I took much pleasure in her visits.

"Nothing has changed here, as you see," I said to her one day, "and nothing ever will as long as I can prevent it."

"Yes," was her only reply. She was a very old lady, very straight, but thin to excess; and although it was crisscrossed with fine wrinkles, her regular face was still beautiful. She looked me straight in the face. I told her how I was in a state of inner harmony, that the life I was leading was the only one suitable for me, and that if I could go on being of use to Colette to the end, in the same place where . . .

To my surprise, Madame Laure interrupted me.

All that remained of her Russian accent was the rolling *r* and a way of overarticulating. "You ought to marry again," she said bluntly.

Such a remark coming from her, attached as she was to memories to the point of making a fetish of them, and coming too after what I had just told her, so astonished me that I could do nothing but shake my head in disagreement.

In the same even voice, she went on: "There is still time for you to have a child."

I felt a wave of repulsion. "My dear Madame Laure, there could be no question of such a thing," I said with some vehemence. "Think what you are saying."

She stood up. I went with her to the door. She walked slowly, but without weakness. At the front door she turned, held out her slender, dry hand, and, determined to spare me nothing at all, she added, "I have only said what Colette would have said to you."

"Stupid old woman," I muttered, going back to my desk.

A year later, when circumstances, a lively mutual inclination, prudence, my duty towards life, everything urged me to begin a new chapter, I still held out; but no doubt my subconscious mind had other views on the matter.

She who is now joined to me, "for better, for worse," will not be at all surprised that there is so little mention of her here. There seems to me no point whatever in singing her praises: the title of this book does that well enough.

Our meeting, like every other meeting, was the result of a series of chances whose rightful sequence could have been upset by the merest breath. At the end of July 1957 I had still not made any arrangements for spending my summer. I really felt very little inclination to leave the rue de Beaujolais, but it was quite essential to behave like everybody else, if only to provide Pauline with a holiday. Having set about it so late, I could scarcely hope to find anywhere to stay except some very big hotel, where there would be a great deal of coming and going; and even then, I should need to pull some kind of a wire. I thought of Maurice Carrère, that charming dandy of the hotel and restaurant trade, the power behind the throne at Maxim's, who that year was all-powerful at the Hôtel du Palais at Biarritz. One telephone call assured me of bed and board. Indeed, Carrère, whom I had known for years, seeing that I was quite alone, took it into his head to find amusements for me. I had scarcely arrived before he took me with him to a charity gala. Overwhelmed by the noise and the brilliant light, I could not make out any face I knew; then suddenly someone rose from his table and opened his arms: it was Lucien Lelong.

Lucien Lelong, whose personality made so strong a mark in the world of fashionable clothes for so long, had been Colette's friend before he became mine. In 1933 she drew a portrait of him that has not appeared before. Here it is:

He is a youthful man, shaped like a capital T.

No one can escape from the way he is built. In the human species, there are those who are shaped like an S—the supple spine, the old and patient cunning of the original serpent. The C is rather better; he curls in upon himself, thrusts forward his gargoyle's head, leans, and holds up—do but think of Briand!—a weight that can crush. Let us pass the D's, those great bloated bellies; we will step prudently aside to avoid the man shaped like an H, who goes straight forward, his shoulders squared, caring for nothing; we will ignore I, a tall creature with a little head and a smaller brain . . . Lucien Lelong is shaped like a T.

What shall I add to so succinct and full a portrait? Don't you see that Lucien Lelong swings surprisingly broad shoulders above a body fined down—bone and muscle—to the essentials?

When he runs—and he is always running, on foot, by car, by motorboat—he leans forward, the better to cut his way through the air with his shoulders, and with the arms of the T. The whole of his small, dogged person tells that he

> T*oils, that he is* T*enacious,* T*hickset, that he*
> T*ries many ventures. "I shall*
> T*riumph!" he cries wordlessly.*
> T*emerarious, he takes over America, and America murmurs,*
> *"Dear me, such* T*emper! That must be good steel!"*

Sometimes he tries to rest . . . He brings a lack of experience and a touching awkwardness to it. But at least during these short truces he can be examined in detail. It is then that one notices that this T, T*urbulent* T*actician*, has two pale-blue eyes that confess, "I am T*ender and* T*rue . . ."*

Lucien Lelong had retired from dress designing ten years before and had bought a very fine estate called

Courbois, at Anglet, just next to Biarritz, and he no longer came to Paris except on rare occasions. So we had lost touch with one another. I might go so far as to say that our friendship had grown cooler because of misunderstandings—each having mistaken for unfeelingness what was in fact meant to be tactful silence. And perhaps I should not have thought of calling on Lucien either, because I had been told, quite wrongly, that he lived very much by himself, whereas on the contrary he kept open house and had masses of friends. But there he was before me: our years of shared memories flashed into our minds and we embraced one another most cordially.

A few years earlier, Lucien Lelong had married a young woman thirty years younger than himself: this was Sanda Dancovici, the child of a Romanian father and a French mother. I had met her twice, the second time at Monte Carlo, where the four of us, Colette, Lucien, she, and I, had luncheon together. I remembered a beautiful, rather hard face, and a self-assurance that may have been a mask for shyness; but Colette had watched her very closely, with a not entirely benevolent attention. Colette's premonitions were sometimes so astonishing that I shall take care to make no inferences from this fact.

Sanda Lelong was a member of the gala committee

and she was busy elsewhere, but she joined us a few minutes later. When, long after, I asked her whether, on seeing me again, she had felt that stirring of the heart that every man thinks he deserves, she told me that all she remembered was the feeling that now she would have to work out another luncheon party at her house, the fourth in a row.

I took to visiting Courbois very often, for I was touched by the kindly welcome I received there. Presently a friendship sprang up between Sanda Lelong and me. There were obstacles enough along our road —and the thirty years that also separated me from her seemed to me by no means the least of them—for us to think that there was no danger in it. Lucien went to bed early, for his health was shaky—or at least he thought it was, which is just as damaging. Sometimes I sat up alone with Sanda. She detected the heaviness of my heart under my unconcerned appearance, and she encouraged me to speak of my unhappiness; I did indeed unburden myself, and I found a great relief in doing so. But suddenly there was a strange, awkward silence between us: I got up and hurriedly took my leave.

I spent Christmas and New Year's at Courbois, but I refused an invitation for Easter: an honorable feeling can preserve you from certain errors, but absence works even better. I set off for a rather dismal journey in Italy, dragging boredom along with me, and a dull rebellion against the renunciations that I was forcing upon myself.

The very evening of my return, on May 9, I telephoned Courbois. All was well there. Very early the next morning I was suddenly awakened: a friend of both of us telephoning to tell me from Sanda that Lucien had died, sleeping beside her, that night. I was quite overcome, and before traveling down for the funeral I sent Sanda a long telegram. As he wished it, Lucien Lelong rests in the little country cemetery at Anglet, far from all traffic and noise, he who for so long had led the dance in Paris.

Courbois was a big eighteenth-century house in the middle of a fifteen-acre park—too big for Sanda to think of keeping it on, particularly as she would have had to buy it back from Lucien's natural heirs. She decided to return to Paris, where she had always lived, and she came up several times to look for a flat. We went out together.

We were both of us free; there were no obstacles left between us; yet I was obliged to admit that the awkwardness that I felt in Sanda's presence was still there. It was only the reasons for it that had changed. Scruples no longer came into it. Sitting there beside her, in a restaurant or in a car, with her knee touching mine, no doubt I had but to make a gesture. It was not only man's usual presumptuousness that convinced me of this, but also that indefinable something that tells one, even when one is with the most reserved of women, that one will not be repulsed. Yes, but this gesture committed my future, giving it a turn that I did not choose to see it take. Sanda was too important a person, and the feeling that I had for her was too serious, for there to be any question of a passing affair between us. This bond that already meant so much to me had to be broken. I was more than ever determined to carry on with my vigil in the rue de Beaujolais until the end, and I was only waiting for an occasion to tell Sanda of this determination.

We had had dinner together. That June evening was so stiflingly hot that we went off to the Bois de Boulogne to look for some less second-hand air. I asked Sanda, who was driving, to stop the car. Without any kind of precaution, I told her of my feelings for her: and that, I said, was why we had to part. For I belonged entirely to my past, and everything was over for me. All I had to offer her youth was the spectacle of the slow decay of a man who would have nothing of the future. I spoke for a long while. She listened to me in silence. As I unfolded my arguments, I became

aware that I was primarily trying to convince myself
and that I was not succeeding at all. A brand-new
heart was beating in me: all my doubts as to the right
way of following Colette's lead gathered themselves
together and argued against me. My breathing obeyed
the rhythm of a kind of inner music. I glanced furtively at Sanda and I saw her bosom rise. Her hands,
all that the beam from the nearby street lamp touched
upon, made two patches of light on the steering
wheel. I turned away my eyes, telling myself that at all
costs I must break the connection or it would be too
late. But I had no sooner uttered the fatal word
"never" than, giving myself the lie straight in the
teeth, I took Sanda in my arms.

The great actor Lucien Guitry, Sacha's father, was
naturally a very witty man, and his pointed remarks
are often more striking than his son's. One October
day when he was strolling about the garden of his
place just outside Paris he stopped before a chestnut
tree: it was one of those that are deceived by the mild-
ness of the autumn or have some kind of fever in their
sap and display new leaves here and there, tenderer
than those of spring, and candles like so many flames.
"He is flowering again," he observed to Marthe
Brandès, his wife; and she heard him add the aside:
"The fool!"

This was merely the quip of a man who, for his part, was continually coming into fresh bloom. As I had at last agreed to turn my face towards the future, I owed it to myself to carry it through to the end—that is, to create the future. It was not without hesitation that I did so, for I had sometimes been much shocked by the difference in age between a father and a small child. But nature has other views, and she grants most men, right until the end, the power of passing on the life they have received. Besides, all my life long I had been much too given to reflection not to end up by taking only those fortunate decisions that run directly counter to common sense!

The birth of a child is the most ordinary thing in the world and the most astonishing. I imagine that to young people, who are less apt to be wonder-struck, it seems natural. For them it forms part of the usual course of events, and they have no time to lose in ecstatic contemplation. But I do absolutely swear to you that the son I was given at the age of seventy-one is the first child that was really worth bringing into existence. I have gazed on this miracle for four years, and day by day I have followed his physical and mental development, careful to let nothing escape me, and understanding precious little after all. It must be stated that of all the children that have been produced up to the present, he is the most forward and the most gifted: modesty prevents me from speaking of his beauty, for he takes after me. He may owe me his life, but he has certainly repaid the obligation, for between a man who has no child and a man who does have one, there is a prodigious difference—the one is strictly limited to himself; the other is carried on, branched, diversified, opened to the worlds of the future.

The circumstances of this bringing-forth were so remarkable that they deserve to be told in detail. Colette used to maintain that when a writer is weak enough to take his own children as the matter for a book, then dotage is breathing down his neck. My particular dotage is sufficiently far along for me not to mind that risk: furthermore, I am not a writer. When, at half past three in the night of December 9, 1960, therefore, Sanda woke me and said, "I think this is it," I was seized by an exceedingly powerful emotion which expressed itself in these words: "Give me a moment to shave, and I am with you." Great events require that nothing should be overlooked; and the man who presents himself before his fate in an unshaved condition does so in an undeniable state of inferiority.

Let me tell those who might not otherwise suspect it that in Paris and the immediately surrounding district—and possibly elsewhere—there are establishments known as maternity homes, where babies are mass-produced, like chicks in an incubator. It was towards one of these factories in Boulogne-sur-Seine that a taxi took us through a deserted, ice-bound and snow-encrusted Neuilly. Already, in the taxi itself, a being of less than naught years old was pertinaciously trying to make its way through to life. In the maternity home everything was at blood-heat. Nurses were hurrying about: doors opened and closed with a muffled sound. The distant squealing of babies rasped the silence. To tell the truth, I was terrified. I had directed all my attention towards the marvels that I expected from this birth, and I had overlooked the surgical, hospital side of it. Now, with the vague chemical smells coming to the help of my keen morning hunger, my heart was sickened rather than moved.

Yet I had read enough popular novels to be acquainted with the way fathers are supposed to wait for long, tormented hours, and I had provided myself with a quantity of cigarettes that would enable me to face it, however long it might last. I wanted a son very much indeed. Not to carry on a name—considerations of that kind meant nothing to me—but to raise up at least one creature that should be like me and whose reactions I might be able to foresee. I should not have had much notion of how to deal with a daughter: the enigma of women, I told myself, must surely come into play at the tenderest years. So when a nurse approached me and uttered these memorable words, "You may come along, monsieur; it is all right," I did not ask her anything about the sex of "it," so that the ambiguity might persist, even if only for a moment. But the obstetrician who had delivered her, a friend, was coming to meet me, and he said, "You have a fine boy: he weighs just over seven pounds, the average Frenchman's weight." I fell on his neck, and the rest of the way to the delivery ward I was walking on air.

The door of the room was open and "it," piping with all the strength of its little lungs, met my ears before my eyes. With a rapid glance I made sure that this Sagittarius was indeed provided with the little arrow that I had been promised, and then, more calmly, that the rest was all there. Not so much as the curled rim of his ears was missing; not so much as a single nail on his toes. The consignment was perfect, only his little head seemed to me a trifle short of hair. I thought him perfectly charming in spite of the sour face with which he showed his disapproval of the way they were treating him. Indeed, they were handling him pretty roughly, slapping him, rubbing him, and holding him upside down. I too thought of protesting against this lack of respect for my son; but I did not presume.

For my part, I must have made a tolerably good impression upon him, for he scarcely had his eyes open when a few days later he directed his first toothless smile towards me. Since then we have been the best possible friends. For the moment he displays no other ambition than that of being like Papa and behaving like Papa; and the only rival that I am aware of is Robin Hood.

Naturally there are times when I cannot repress a certain uneasiness, one that arises from many causes. In the first place, shall I ever be able to repay this child all that I receive from him? To begin with, I owe him an undeniable renewal of youth. "Young" husband, "young" father: the adjective has a delightful ring to my ears, which had been feeling unfairly deprived of it.

My son does not merely accept me: he seeks me out as a playmate. When we run races and play at wrestling or boxing and roll about on the ground, the sight may perhaps be rather distressing. What does it matter, so long as it is not distressing for him, and so long as my wind and my muscles, called upon for efforts that they no longer thought they could produce, respond to the demand? It is worth noting how much younger than the rest people stay who are forced to make the effort because of professsional obligations or a particular set of desires or some other necessity—actors, conductors, medical men, saleswomen, pederasts, aged young fathers. Retirement, both for the employee and for the big manufacturer, is usually the same as a step towards the grave. "At last I am going to be able to look after myself," they say: and they forget to add, "alas!"

The time will come when the boy goes to school. The home circle which meant everything to him will no longer be his one horizon. He will notice that his father is not like the other boys' fathers, and the word "old age" will take on a meaning for him. It is a danger one has to run. Children try so hard to be like all other children that they will even envy one who has a strawberry mark or lupus on his head; but at the same time they are proud of anything that sets them apart.

And then, has there not always been a particular kind of amity between children and old men, and young people and old men? Nowadays, when there are four years between them the young no longer understand one another. They have a foreboding that the middle-aged man will overwhelm them with advice, hold himself up as an example, and make the most of his superiority. So they avoid the fogy and depend more on the prehistoric fossil. The fossil is at least no longer their rival. He experienced the same problems that they know, and the same conflicts, and since he has reached his present age, he clearly must have got over them.

If the young are quite happy to confide in me, it is because I do my utmost to see their problems from their point of view and not from mine. If a rope of mountain climbers were in difficulties and a man on the top of an alp were to call down to them, "Do as I do. Stretch out in the sun and smoke a cigarette," would it be well received?

I suppose that I shall never be classed in the "old gentleman" category, for I did not set about it early enough: the category of "aged young man" is good enough for me. No young fellow has yet offered me his seat in the métro. It may simply be a question of bad breeding, but I prefer to think that they are prevented from doing so by a certain air that I possess. It still astonishes me when I say *tu* to a young man and he does not reply with the same familiarity. Some do so: thank God, from my point of view, and so much the worse for them. Jean Cocteau seemed to me the pattern of those who refuse to be labeled old men. It is true that you hardly notice the aging of those who are carrying on the process at the same time as yourself, and I had known Jean ever since the little Lycée Condorcet, when we were both twelve. On the other hand, long separations can produce the most disconcerting results. Some years ago I suddenly came across another schoolfellow whom I had not seen since the lycée but whose likeness to the boy in short trousers and a sailor collar was so great that I fell upon his neck crying, "How are you, old fellow! All these years since the sixth form!" The man looked at me coldly, and replied with more point than civility, "You must have been very much behind in your schooling, monsieur, for I am only forty, and it seems to me that you . . ." He then introduced his father, who might perfectly well have been mine, or at least so it seemed to me, and whom I should certainly never have recognized.

Jean Cocteau and I had much the same notions about time and its relative value—not its value as mathematicians understand it—and these we used to discuss for hours on end, walking up and down under the arcades of the Palais-Royal. One day we were talking on the broad walk of the Place du Théâtre-Français, opposite Stock's bookshop, when a girl darted towards Jean, waving a little book. "Monsieur, do you do autographs?" she asked, as if she had been in a dry cleaner's asking, "Do you do accordion pleats?" A few young people of both sexes followed the ingenuous collector's example. Jean did what they asked him with a good grace. After they had gone, he let his smile droop and he said to me, "Do you realize that I have been at the top of the bill like this for more than forty years? If only you knew how tiring it is!" He was silent for a moment, and then added with a sigh, "And I shall certainly have to stay there until the end!" He was aware that being well known was as important to him as the air he breathed; and even more important than the notoriety was the effort he had to make to keep it up.

He and I agreed that the only paradise we could conceive of was a paradise that was in perpetual danger of being lost and that perpetually required to be regained. But although we put heaven and hell on the same footing as the products of human megalomania, we did take pleasure in the notion that time as we measure it is no more than a fraud. That which is to happen has already happened; that which is not yet in existence both is and has ceased to be. Time might just as well be read in one direction as in another; it might just as well go faster or slower. Nothing ever disappears, and it is our life, as we have lived it, that is eternal and that is written down forever in some kind of a way and in some kind of a place. Already we know that messages can reach us from stars that went out thousands of millions of years ago, and that sounds we cannot hear set in motion waves whose significance escapes us. It is not impossible that one day we shall be able to call back the visual and audible past. From there it would be but a step to call upon the future! And perhaps nothing more than a spool run backwards would be enough for us to live our life again, or part of it, or the same life several times over!

Thus I talked about the eternal recommencement with the author of *L'Éternel retour*. Colette and I had lost contact with this sylph, found him again and lost him once more, until the time when, equally attracted, all of us, by the magnetism of the Palais-Royal, we had seen one another without let-up almost every day for fifteen years.

This place so loaded with history, this enchanted quadrangle, the Palais-Royal, haunted by the red robes of two cardinals, more than once filled with rioters, sometimes given over to whores and money-changers, was transformed for a brief moment—too brief—into a nest of friends, bringing together writers and artists of the same spiritual family. The gentle Christian Bérard, with his round head, his flax-blue eyes, his burning beard; Emmanuel Berl, with his brilliant intelligence shining through his faun-like mask (a man for whom friendship is but one of the many tortures he delights in); Mireille, that industrious ant who seems to have swallowed a grasshopper— these formed the minor stars in the constellation Cocteau-Colette. For a short while others joined the band—Pierre Lazareff, the most farseeing of shortsighted men, secreting journalism as others secrete their various humors; Hélène Lazareff, as wayward as a will-o'-the-wisp and provided with antennae for perceiving the invisible; Hervé Mille, who might have been begotten by a demon upon a nautch girl one night when the fiend was feeling tender and the wench enigmatical; and his brother Gérard—alas, the unforgettable Gérard.

The contrast between Colette and Jean Cocteau could scarcely have been greater. What united them was that they were, both the one and the other, exceedingly curious; but they were not curious about the same things. Colette watched; Jean listened, sniffed the wind. He was a hunter, and hidden myths were his quarry; the extraordinary was his ordinary diet. The poetry of the one was in the grass roots; that of the other aimed at the stars. But Colette's probing in the earth reached the soil's heart, whereas Cocteau's flights sometimes went astray. It is not for me to pass judgment on his work; and besides I still see its author too clearly through it. I believe that the magic wand so plainly visible at the end of his long poet's fingers did not prevent the magic from appearing when he summoned it, and that if Jean by no means stripped man's heart bare, he did at least expose its wilder beating.

I have never known anyone with a more agile mind. That is why he was so often and so unfairly called a juggler. The name hurt him; so did the slightest criticism. I drew a sketch of him in *Près de Colette* and I thought I had put a great deal of affection into it. He received me coldly: "Really, you aren't very flattering."

"How can you say such a thing, Jean?"

" 'Through this man, standing there with his halo of gray hair that is beginning to recede from his high forehead,' " he quoted accurately, and added, "Do you think that so very charming?"

This dread of slipping off the platform, even if it should only be for a moment, became an obsession during the last years of his life. There was not an article, not a preface, not a press release that he would refuse to write. Indeed, he burned himself out in this exhausting struggle for the limelight. His last coronary struck him when he had only just finished his own souvenir portrait for television. An admirable piece, his own through and through, and one in which he sought both to make his picture clear and to confuse it, as though he were looking into a reflecting pool that was sometimes motionless and sometimes ruffled by the breeze. It cost him a great deal in labor and anxiety. I went to see him at Milly a couple of days before the misfortune whose consequences carried him off, and he told me about his uneasiness. "I am not sure of having hit the right tone," he said. "I am quite sure you have," I replied with complete sincerity, for I felt that there was nothing more perfectly in Jean's line than that self-portrait.

He did not experience the peace of evening, but it was not made for him. I loved him; there were many of us who wept over his death; and by it the public has lost many a sparkling page, many an audacious drawing. It should not be forgotten that Cocteau had chanced upon this title, *Portraits-Souvenirs*, for one of his most brilliant books: it is no doubt one of the most forgotten of his works, but it is the one posterity will choose when it calls upon this witness of his own age to provide his testimony. He gathered the whole of his frail strength to crown this collection with his own likeness: the links that held everything together broke under the strain, and indeed the whole sequence had very much the look of a theme taken from Cocteau's own world of allegory.

I have a photograph, taken two years ago, of Jean Cocteau holding my son on his knees. Laurent is laughing heartily, Jean is exceedingly grave: I may add that it might just as well have been the other way around. I look at it, and it makes me very thoughtful, for Jean was exactly my age. How much time is left for me to try out the role of educator on this little boy—a role to which I think I am suited? The advantage that we old men possess is that we have seen so many parents go wrong that it seems to us impossible that we should make the same mistakes; the disadvantage is that the lesson may be rather suddenly cut short. The man who dies at a reasonable age (although men rarely feel that it is reasonable at any time) does so at the moment when he has accumulated the greatest amount of knowledge and has had the greatest amount of experience. Nevertheless, I shall have to try to go at least part of the road with this little fellow. I have so much to say to him!

I am well aware that experience is supposed to be incommunicable. Generally speaking, it is true that each generation, under the penalty of sterility, must remake its own; for wisdom has to be acquired, not passively received. And yet, although it is a fact that you only learn by getting burnt, there are still different degrees of burn.

I feel that one can leave the young to find things out for themselves but still one can save them time. Not in the sense that most parents mean it. Out of love for their children, they try to preserve them from the dangers that await them, and to this end they paint mankind in the darkest colors. I believe there is nothing worse than this way of brushing off the bloom from the fruit that these children will have to pick. In order not to fall into this error, I shall only have to remember my own father's teachings and the dreadful effects they had on me.

Throughout the whole of my adolescence, he never wearied of telling me over and over again that money was the one driving power in social life and that getting it and saving it was the sole end of one's existence. As for women, they were, without exception, monsters of cunning and rapacity. Everything about them was false—hair, teeth, bosom, soul. Any of them who might show me a kindness were only after my money, though I did not have two pennies to rub together. That went for most men, too; for almost their only activity consisted of cheating one another.

Does it make good sense to provide a new, weak creature, already troubled by the inhibitions of his age, with such a discouraging picture of what the future has in store for him? My father, and many other fathers too, would have thought it wildly imprudent to look back into his own experience for my advantage and pick out his hours of happiness, affection, generosity—the emotions that make one richer. Yet, that would have been the only way of helping me, for the road the young have to travel is a hard one, and it cost me ten years to rid mine of the brambles that my father, the best and most unselfish of men, had planted in it.

A sort of custom and really perhaps a sense of what is fitting require me to finish this book with some reflections upon death in general and upon my own in particular. I do not feel any urge to do so. I confess that my romanticism does not extend that far. Speculations of this kind are very well for the young Hamlet or the youthful Lamartine in love with Elvire. Chateaubriand already had one foot in the grave when he was about forty; and the other foot, unbiddable, took another forty years to join it there.

It may be that some people will find this free-and-easy manner shocking. Obviously, there is my own family, above all that little boy whom I can hear laughing in the next room and who, as I know very well, will early have no father. Do I, for that reason, have to behave as though he had none already? Must I sink into dismal thoughts about the deprivations that my son will suffer from my death, and hasten that death by doing so?

I have known serenity; I sank into it very gently, as one sinks down into quicksand. I have changed it, thank God, for a fresh commitment. As I had nobody left who loved me, all that remained for me to do was to drift along in life; and this went on until I perceived that letting oneself drift was the same thing as dying. Now, the choice of death is about the only one that I will not allow. We have to wait until we are killed. A microbe, a virus, a tumor, a bursting artery will do the job: let us be satisfied with that!

But the duty of living implies the duty of remaining young as long as possible. It is by no means certain that all men are convinced of this, so many does one see who settle before their time into a most dangerous state of self-neglect. After all, youthfulness cannot be expected to remain in us without some kind of care. Self-control is necessary at any age, and a young man of twenty who abandons himself to flabbiness is already a wretched spectacle.

Do not expect, O my equals, that I shall provide you with any receipt for youthfulness—a receipt smelling of the dispensary. It may be that one day I shall be the first to run to the physicians—perhaps indeed to make a nuisance of myself; but up to the present I have taken no medicines. I maintain that we are ourselves capable of dealing with most of the illnesses that lie in wait for us. Treating them with contempt is not enough. What is called for is a refusal, a stiffening, a revolt that helps the activities of the anti-what-have-you's that are meant to protect us. I know people who go several times a year to have tests and check-ups and so on, to detect any possible nascent illness and nip it in the bud. Nothing on earth would induce me to take it upon myself to dissuade them. But after all they are maintaining a state of anxiety in themselves which is certainly the best ally of what they are trying to avoid. I have many medical men among my friends, and sometimes my family, rendered suspicious and even alarmed by my excellent physical condition, oblige me to go and see them. These are well-known doctors, and they are therefore overworked. My visits to them always end with my granting them a consultation and prescribing a course of treatment based upon optimism and good humor.

Everybody agrees that it is necessary to make one's body obey rules of hygiene; but not everybody asks whether there may not also be rules of mental hygiene. A man who devotes three quarters of an hour every morning to physical jerks, which he usually does badly and which make him low in spirit, never thinks of washing pointless worries out of his mind, together with squalid little calculations and the dregs of low envy and greed that clog him and harm the sound functioning of his alimentary tract, heart, and nervous system.

But cleaning out one's batteries is not enough; they also have to be recharged. Just as one's cares and worries foul up one's organs, so, necessarily, there are states that favor their rejuvenation. A single word defines them all: happiness. So long as the quest for it is not regarded as the most imperative duty, its practice taught in the schools, and its name carved upon even the smallest pediments, the future of the human race will still be in jeopardy.

While you are waiting for youth to return, do your best not to age too fast.

Never say, "I am weary." Spare yourself the weariness.

Do, on the other hand, say, "When I am old," and keep thinking of it as a remote eventuality up to a very advanced age.

Firmly believe that you look young. How do you

expect to be able to convince others if you do not believe it yourself? And this belief will in fact rejuvenate you. I have made up my mind once and for all that because of some inexplicable phenomenon all looking glasses and all photographs make me look older. I also avoid looking in a mirror that will show me from behind, for I suspect that a clearing may have appeared in the forest of my hair, and I would rather not know about it.

Every time people tell you that you are "astonishingly young" for your age, do not take it as a piece of set politeness but as the statement of a blindingly obvious truth. Only, one must keep the words "for his age" from being tagged on to everything that is said about what one does. "How active he is"—we know that inevitably, with an axe-like fall, there will come these three syllables, quite without value in human speech: "for his age." Why not simply say, "He plays tennis well, he runs well, his voice is firm"? By no means the least important savings are those of words.

Do not let your curiosity grow dull. If you see things less clearly, look at them with more attention.

Watch your speech and do not let it slow down. Yet there must be no obvious effort, for be warned—almost everything a man does to make himself young after a certain period in his life ages him. If he tries to force a free and easy manner, all he does is to empha-size his slowness and the creaking of his joints. Still less effective is that way of dwelling upon one's years in order to provoke contradiction: "You may well im-agine that at my advanced age . . ." Playing the old man for fun, imitating the voice, stance, grin is quite disastrous; few recover from it. Dyeing one's hair is utterly forbidden: it is always obvious; it makes the wrinkles deeper and hardens the features. Trying to make oneself look youthful by wearing bright colors in town when the young happily wear dark suits to look older is the act of a fool.

Is all this mere trifling? No: it is good manners. Good manners require one to show the people around one, and the rest of the world, the least saddening ap-pearance that one can manage. I know nothing more moving than some very old married couples who have kept a mutual desire to please and who have therefore by no means let themselves go. And it may well be that they owe their long life to these little daily re-straints, this exercise of self-control.

From where I sit, I can hear the outcry that receives my words. "The delights of growing old—it is easy enough for you to talk, you who . . ." This means that I am not a pauper or even economically distressed. I entirely agree, and I am perfectly aware of what old age can mean in the way of distress for them. It is also true that I enjoy excellent health, and I am bold enough to write these words without knocking on wood.

I hope with all my heart that social legislation is making the lot of needy old people better and that it will go on doing so. A character in some comedy by Flers and Caivallet says roughly this: "I cannot bear the poor. Therefore I give them all the money I can, so that they shall not be poor any longer." My political ideas are still vague and unsure, but I, too, vote for the total abolition of the poor. Yet I do not feel that talking about happiness as I have done throughout this essay is insulting the unfortunate. When we were lying in the straw in the camp at Compiègne, one of my companions in starvation and I composed splendid imaginary meals before going to sleep.

"I don't agree," said my friend. "With the *canard aux olives* I would rather have a Chambertin."

Oaths, accompanied by threats, burst out all around. "Shut up! I can't bear it any longer. Don't you think it is bad enough? How would you like me to stop your gob with the heel of my boot? Sadists!"

Yet, my fellow prisoner and I did find our hunger eased by these theoretical feasts. We presumed to look upon our misfortune with a humorous eye, believing that there was no other manner of battling against it. Many people thought our way unseemly. Dramatics are always so well received!

I cannot tell how I shall behave when aches and decrepitude come, or that illness which will thrust me, roughly or not so roughly, out of this world. I have nothing to say against tasting a pleasure in advance; but it does not seem to me sensible to dwell upon unpleasant things before they have even happened. I only beg that I may, without weakening, remain true to the oaths that I have inwardly sworn; honor the life dwelling within me to its very last; and even if only a spark remains to me, treat it still as a holy flame.

Maurice Goudeket

Maurice Goudeket (1889-1977) was a French businessman and man of letters. He is best known as the author of *Close to Colette* (1957), a biography of the celebrated author to whom he was married for twenty years. After Colette's death, M. Goudeket married Sanda Lelong, with whom he had a son in 1960.